CABELL COUNTY

VIRGINIA/WEST VIRGINIA

MINUTE

BOOK

1809-1815

*Combining Surviving
Court Minutes & Law Orders*

Carrie Eldridge

HERITAGE BOOKS
2010

HERITAGE BOOKS

AN IMPRINT OF HERITAGE BOOKS, INC.

Books, CDs, and more—Worldwide

For our listing of thousands of titles see our website
at
www.HeritageBooks.com

Published 2010 by
HERITAGE BOOKS, INC.
Publishing Division
100 Railroad Ave. #104
Westminster, Maryland 21157

Other Heritage Books by the author:
Cabell County's Empire for Freedom
Minute Books: Cabell County, [West] Virginia Minute Book 1, 1809–1815

*Miscellaneous Cabell County, West Virginia Records: Order Book Overseers of the Poor, 1814–1861;
Fee Book, 1826–1839; 1857–1859 (Rule Book); Cabell Land for Tax Purposes, 1861–1865*

Nicholas County, Kentucky Property Tax Lists, 1800–1811 with Indexes to Deed Books A & B (2), and C

*Nicholas County, Kentucky Records: Stray Book 1, 1805–1811; Stray Book 2, 1813–1819;
Stray Book 3, 1820–1870; and Execution Book A, 1801–1878*

Torn Apart: How Cabell Countians Fought the Civil War

International Standard Book Numbers
Paperbound: 978-1-58549-875-8
Clothbound: 978-0-7884-8523-7

1809-1815

CABELL COUNTY MINUTE BOOK

ABSTRACTS

An abstract of the combinded "First" Minute and
Law Order Books of Cabell County, VA/WV

	sq.mi.	1809	1842	1867
CABELL	282			
Lincoln	439			721
Wayne	508		1229	
Logan	456	2109		
Mingo	424			

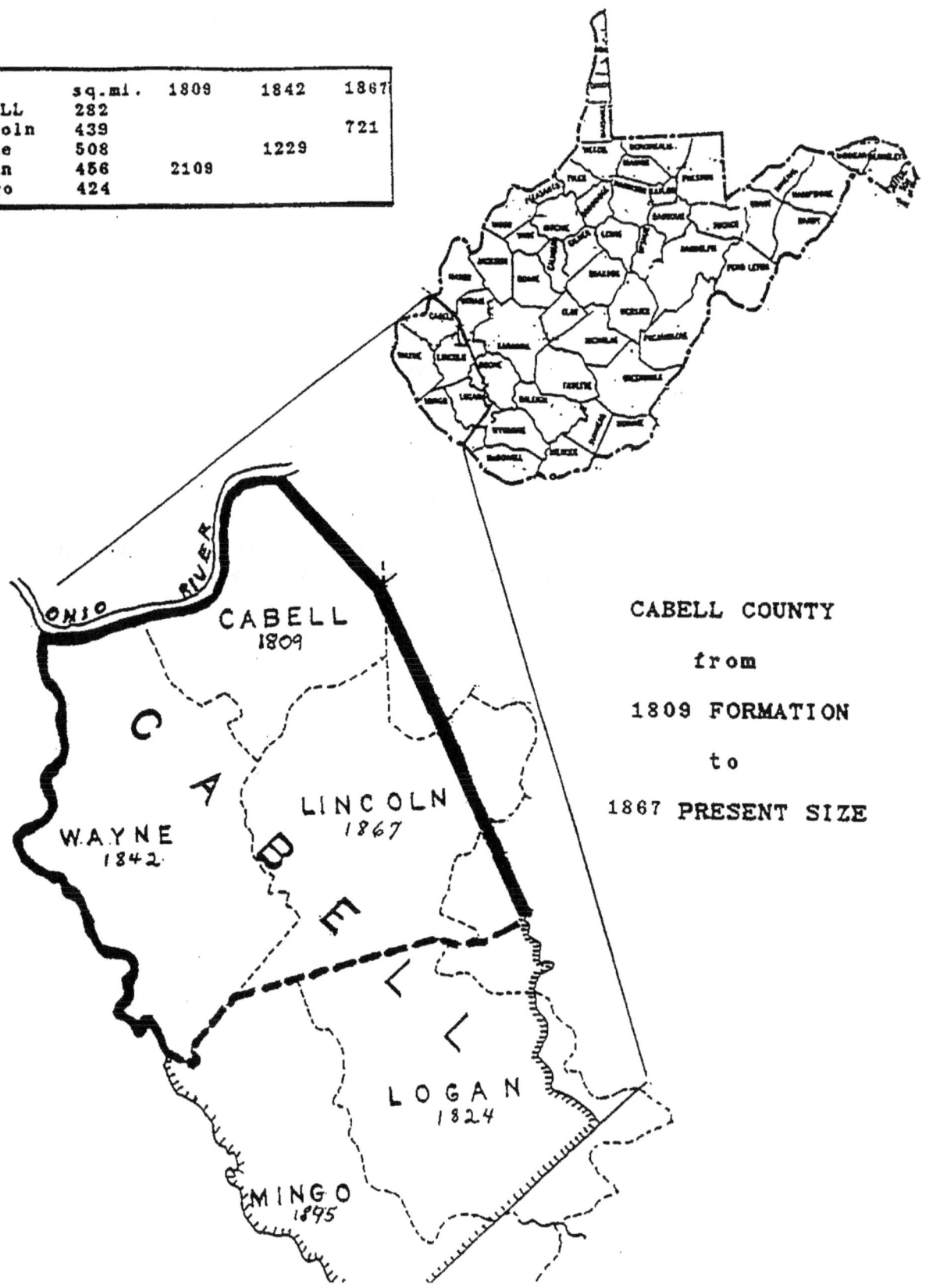

OHIO RIVER

CABELL 1809

WAYNE 1842

LINCOLN 1867

CABELL

LOGAN 1824

MINGO 1895

CABELL COUNTY

from

1809 FORMATION

to

1867 PRESENT SIZE

CONTENTS

A Book with many uses   4

Abbreviations   5

Abstract of Minutes   6-43

Jury Duty Frequency   44-50

Index   51-57

A BOOK WITH MANY USES

NOTE: The "Minute Book 1809-1815" is the normal
small ledger book common to court houses,
but it has been used for different enteries
on three separate occasions.

        *

pp 1-184 are the actual Minute Book.

        x

pp 185-255 are a section of the Cabell County
Rule Book for July 1865 to May 1866.
        x

pp 256-308 represent the pay roster for the
"Washington Aqueduct".

   The material in the two later sections will be
abstracted at a later date.

*

My numbering because the book is only partially numbered.
Some pages are double pages with a single number because
the material is on two pages.(See page 143)

MINUTE BOOK FOR CABELL COUNTY SUPERIOR COURT 1809-1815

cross reference from Law Order Books for complete names
Law Order 1809-1812 = pp 1-56
Law Order 1812-1819 = pp 57-141
(see separate cover for 1815-1819)

LO (abbreviation for Law Orders)   tres-trespass
AB-assault and battery   gaming-illegal game of chance
al-and others   liquor-selling liquor no license
clk-clerk

Many of the entries in these books are difficult to read either due to poor hand writing, bad ink or abbreviations. By comparing these books and other information from the same period most of the names are correct. No attempt has been made to provide the complete word for word entry because:

1. Most entries are duplicated many times as cases are continued.
2. The clerk does not always complete the original information.
3. The clerk's short hand often makes no sense.

An effort HAS been made to include all the names recorded and the case information if listed.

Three quarter of the cases are either debt(by bond,contract or convenant) or AB (assualt & battery with or without trespass). The AB cases seem to appear after the elections and at the same time as indictments for selling liquor without a license(probably fights as the result of too much alcohol).
There is one case of murder,one for larceny and several for ejectment(remove land holders due to overlapping land claims caused by Virginia's metes and bounds land system).
Possibly the most interesting part of these court cases is the amount of money involved. Many cases are called for less than fifty dollars, indicating that going to court was a method of entertainment.

Names are rendered as recorded unless a single letter is questioned (1 or e) then the most common spelling is accepted.

CABELL COUNTY MINUTE BOOK 1809-1815

NOTE: plantiff appears first - defendant second
each case entry is indented
jury trials are separated

pg 1--------
- At the house of Wm.MERRITT 2nd Monday after the 4th Monday in April 1809 Commonwealth of Viriginia Cabell County
  Present JOHN COALTER Judge of Superior Court appointing Edmund MORRIS clerk of court,who with John MORRIS SR.,Thomas BUFFINGTON, Jerrimah WARD,Manoah BOSTICK,John RUSSELL, & Jesse SPURLOCK go bond of $10,000 for clerk
- James WILSON atty qualified for prosecutor for Commonwealth
- Deed of bargain & sale Edmund McGINNIS & wife(Sally)
    to Manoah BOSTICK
- Botetourt   1st Monday in April   - 1st Monday in September
  Monroe   2nd Monday in April   2nd Monday in September
  Greenbrier 3rd Monday   "   3rd Monday   "
  Kanawha   4th Monday   "   4th Monday   "
  Mason   1st Mon. after the 4th Mon.in Apr. & Sep.
  Cabell   2nd Mon. after the 4th Mon.in Apr. & Sep.

pg 2------
- Deed from Daniel WITCHER & wife(Sally)
    to Manoah BOSTICK sent to Greenup
  County Kentucky
- Alex.PORTER,Stephen KELLY,Isom GARRETT,& Robert TABOR finded for
    not attending Gran Jury
- David CARTMILL,Henry HUNTER qualify to practice law
Grand Jury~Elisha McCOMAS foreman,Benjamin GARRETT,Thomas BUFFINGTON,David McCOMAS,Jonathan BUFFINGTON,David DOUTHAT,Thomas CLAP,Henry BROWN,Mark RUSSELL,Michael HOLLAND,William FULLERTON,Lerose MERRITT,Joseph HILYARD,Charles ALSBURY,Samuel FERGUSON,Peter LOWER,Charles BOOTH, & John FERGUSON--
return: against William JORDEN & Andrew JORDEN indictment-nusance
        against James B(torn)(see pg4) BEAR & Obadiah MERRITT
pg 3   (LO says Bias& Biars))   for an affray
----   "   Chester HOW living in fornication with Nancy DROWN
          "   Nancy DROWN living in fornication with Chester HOW
          "   John RODGERS adultry with Jane FULLERTON
          "   Jane FULLERTON adultry with John RODGERS
          "   Joshua JONES living in fornication with Polly
                         BARNHEART
          "   Polly BARNHEART   same   Joshua JONES
          "   Thomas WARD   retailing spirtuous liquors-no license
          "   Thomas KILGORE   same
          "   Samuel SHORT   same
          "   William MERRITT   same
          "   William HOLDERBY   same
          "   John SIMMONS   same
          "   Richard CRUMP   same
          "   William GREENWOOD   same----
- William JORDEN & Andrew JORDEN, James BEARS, Obadiah BEARS, Obadiah
    MERRITT & others -summoned before Grand Jury-
Pg4--------

```
-  etc.( each case indicted is summoned)
-    Deed from John MORRIS SR. & wife PEGGY to Edmund MORRIS
-    deed from Edmund MORRIS 7 wife SALLY  to Manoah BOSTICK
-    James WILSON prosecutor allowed $5 for 1 day service
-    Edmund MORRIS clerk allowed $10 for services for term
-    Thomas WARD  sheriff allowed $8
pg 5        9 oct 1809 house of William MERRITT-John COALTER judge-
         first causes(see pg 2)
Grand Jury retired:Manoah BOSTICK,Henry BROWN,Mark RUSSELL,Thomas CLAP,
Alexander PORTER,Stephen KELLY,David DAVIS,Elisha McCOMAS,James
HOLDERBY,Nathaniel SCALES,James JORDEN Sr.,Thomas KILGORE,Michael
HOLLAND,Lerose MERRITT,George SPURLOCK,George HOLLENBACK,Charles
ALSBURY,Peter LOWER,Joseph HILYARD
-    Wm.H.CAVENDISH,John MATHEWS,Ballard SMITH,Silvester WOODWARD,Lewis
         SUMMERS qualified to practice law
-    Isaac HUTCHINSON clk of Superior Court Monroe County $3.8
-    Commonwealth  plf v James BEARS,OBIDIAH BEARS,OB.MERRITT-atty
         D.CARTMILL   rule for prosecutor(James WILSON) - for costs
pg 6---------
-    Alex.CATLETT Jr. prosecutor for commonwealth $30
-    Commonwealth  vs  Wm.& ANDREW JORDEN  plead not guilty
-    EVANS & al  plf        (LO p10) Thomas EVANS, James LOCKHEART assee
         vs                        of John WOODWARD
     HAMPTON     cont.  ( Henry HAMPTON,Henry BROWN & Reuben SLAUGHTER)
Pg 7-----
-    Grand Jury returns:
     JAMES HOGAN for    Tresspass
     THOMAS CHAPMAN     adultry with Jane Ferguson
     JANE FERGUSON      fornication with Thomas Chapman
     SARAH HOLLAND      a free mulatto- fornication with PETER a Negro
                        man of William TONEY'S
-    ALEX.PORTER & ISOM GARRAT fines receded for not app.Grand Jury
-    JESSE SPURLOCK & JAMES TURILY(?) SAME
adjourned  until 10 O'ck
pg 8        Tuesday 10 oct 1809 (same judge as yesterday---------
-    MARK RUSSELL summoned to show cause
-    JAMES HOGAN summoned to answer indictment
-    Commonwealth vs Thomas WARD  liquor no license  dismissed for cost
-    same with:John.SIMMONS-WILLIAM MERRITT, WILLIAM HOLDERBY, Richard
         CRUMP(p 12)
pg 9-----------
-    Commonwealth vs  Saml.SHORT   filed & cont.
-    same     vs  Thos.KILGORE  same
-    same     vs  William GREENWOOD same
-    commth   vs  Chester HOW     to show cause at next
-    same     vs  N. DROWN        same
-    same     vs  J.RODGERS       same
-    same     vs  J.FULLERTON     same
-    same     vs  J.JONES         same
-    same     vs  P.BARNHEART     same
-----------------------------------------
-    James MOOMAN & al(wife) vs  Wm.TONEY  tres & AB
Jury called: Thomas CLAP,Philip WINCE,William GREENWOOD,
```

Zach STEPHENSON, Elisha McCOMAS, James TORGA, James BEARS, Alex CATLET
Jr., Saml. BLUE, Gilbert STEPHENSON, William LOVE, & Benj. GARRETT Jr.
pg 10
- Thomas WARD vs John HANNAN to show cause
- John MORRIS ordered to appear

-Superior Court-house of William S. MERRITT 7 may 1810 Judge John COALTER
-Grand Jury: Edmd. McGINNIS, Joseph HILYARD, Charles ALSBURG, Danl. DOUTHAT,
Thos. CLAP, Charles BOOTH, Wm. FULLERTON, Robert WILSON, William FURGUSON,
Peter LOWER, Thomas KILGORE, James JORDEN Sr., George SPURLOCK, William
JORDEN, Lerose MERRITT, Saml. FURGUSON.

- Thomas L. PRESTON qualified atty
- James BEARS, Obadiah BEARS, Obadiah MERRIT sent before jury
---
- Commth vs Saml. SHORT selling liquor without license
Jury called: James WILSON, David NIXS, Allen RECE, Peter SCALES, William
GREENWOOD, David McCOMAS, Isaac RUSSELL, Reuben SLAUGHTER, John
RUSSELL, Wm. BUFFINGTON, Saml. NEAL, Jesse SPURLOCK (def. guilty)

- fined for not attending Grand Jury
Stephen KELLY, Martin HALL, Elisha McCOMAS, Alex. PORTER, William WALKER &
Jesse SPURLOCK excused.

- Commth vs James BEARS, Obadiah BIARS, Obdadiah MERRIT for affary
Jury: Peter DIRTING, Robert HOLDERBY, James HOGAN, Reuben BOOTON, Isaac
HATFIELD, John BURTON, David HOGAN, Obadiah HARRISON, John SIMMONS, Gilbert
STEPHENSON, James MORMANS & John BARNER Verdict for plf.

- John FURGUSON fined $2 contempt
- M. BOSTICK vs W. MERRITT asser Thos. ERVIN McCOMAS pleaded
page 12 Tuesday 8th May 1810 Same judge as yesterday
- Commth vs BIARS on indictment-judgement accordingly

- Commth vs William JORDEN & Andrew JORDEN
Jury: James BIARS, William GREENWOOD, Obadiah MERRITT, Elisha McCOMAS,
Chester HOW, James MORMAN, Samuel NEAL, John RODGERS, Peter DIRTING, William
FULLERTON, Isaac HATFIELD, Daniel NEAL. def not guilty

- Commth vs Thos. KILGORE selling spirtuous liquor no license
Jury: James REA, Benjamin GARRETT, Reuben SLAUGHTER, Malchor STROOP, John
MORRIS Jr., William BUFFINGTON, Richard BROWN, Peter BARNHEART, Thomas
CLAP, James FORD, John GRIFFITH, John FERGUSON. not guilty
---
page 13-----
- Commth vs Dan(Wm.) GREENWOOD same jury-not guilty
- Commth vs James HOGAN Henry HAMPTON Jr. prosecutor def for costs
- Commth vs Chester HOW information filed
- same vs Nancy DROWN same
- Commth vs John RODGERS show cause
- Commth vs Jane FULLERTON show cause---
- Thos. EVANS & al vs R. SLAUGHTER debt/ Manoah BOSTICK Sp D for R.
page 14----
- Commth vs J. JONES adultry with Barnheart cause & discharged

- same vs P.BARNHEART forn. with Jones
- same vs J.FERGUSON forn. with Chapman
- same vs Thos.CHAPMAN adultry with Frerguson
- same vs Sarah HOLLAND(free negro)
- commth vs Saml.SHORT return to court to hear verdict
Court adjourned till tomorrow 9 O'clk
- Commth vs John MORRIS Jr. information taken -plead not guilty
- Thomas WARD vs John HANNAN (Charles ALSBURY & William MORRIS)
Judgement set aside & declaration filed desposition of John SHELTON &
Noah SCALES
pg 15-------
- Superior Court 10 oct at Court House- Judge John COALTER
Grand Jury:David McCOMAS,Elisha McCOMAS,Thos.CLAP,Chester HOW,Mark
RUSSELL,Nath. SCALES,Wm.BUFFINGTON,Michl.HOLLAND,John MORRIS Sr.,Jesse
SPURLOCK,Chas.LOVE,George SPURLOCK,Edmund McGINNIS,Manoah BOSTICK, Thos.
BUFFINGTON,James JORDEN,Jacob HITE,Sampson SANDERS,Wm.DINGESS,Chas.
ALSBURY,Thos. KILGORE.

- Saml.SHORT & security Saml.SMILEY petioned court
    $100 and good behavior for one year
- Commth vs Chester HOW dismissed for costs
- SAME Nancy DROWN same
- Allen TAYLOR sworn to practice law
page 16---
- commth vs Obadiah MERRITT plea not guilty
- Noah SCALES,John RODGERS,David SPURLOCK fined
- Daniel RUFFNER assee (of J.L.RUFFNER) vs John BARRET(& John
    REYNOLDS) debt WIT:Thomas WARD
Court adjourned till oct 10 - Tuesday 9 oct 1810 same judge
- Commth vs John MORRIS Jr. (libel) information
- Manoah BOSTICK vs William MERRIT debt/ information
page 17--
- (Thomas)EVAN & al(James LOCKHEART assee of John WOODWARD)
        vs H.HAMPTON(Henry BROWN & Reubin SLAUGHTER) IN debt
- Richard CRUMP ordered to Appear
- Chester HOW fined $2 not appearing Grand Jury
- Thomas WARD vs John HANNAH & al(Charles ALSBURY & Wm.MORRIS)
        Cont at cost of def
- Henry HAMPTON vs James HOGAN AB
- Manoah BOSTICK vs William MERRITT case
Page 18------
- A deed from Chester HOW & NANCY his wife to Stephen SPURLOCK
Superior Court 6 may 1811 Judge John Coalter

-Grand Jury:Manoah BOSTICK,Sampson SANDERS,Jacob HITE,Daniel DOUTHAT,
Patent WALKER,Jacob FUDGE,Isom HANNAN,Joseph HILYARD,John Mc MAHAN,John
GRIFFITH,Thomas CLAP,William BUFFINGTON,John FURGUSON,James GRAY, Jesse
McCOMAS,John HATFIELD,William FULLERTON

- James J.MAYERS qualified atty.
- Henry HAMPTON,John HANNON, Chester HOW,Lawerence BRYANT,Robert
RUTHERFORD,Thomas McCOMAS failed to attend jury
- Edmund MORRIS,bond for clerk(by John MORRIS Sr.,Thos.BUFFINGTON,
Jeremiah WARD,Manoah BOSTICK,John RUSSELL,Jesse SPURLOCK

Pg 19----------
-      a deed of partition from Garrett PAYTON and wife(Agatha STROTHER)
       to John H.PAYTON and wife(Susannah SMITH)- Charles TAYLOR
         Clk. of Montgomery court
-      James HOLDERBY called as wittness
-      commth. vs Samual SHORT failed to attend Grand JURY
-      commth vs Sander WITCHER not guilty and bon
-      commth. vs. Daniel NEIL AB not guilty and cond.
-      commth vs Daniel WITCHER Jr. not guilty and cont.
-      commth. vs. John BYERS AB Alias Summons awarded
-      commth. vs. Charles STUART AB not guilty and cont
-      commth vs. Moses MOTT assualt sops. awarded
-      commth vs. Hugh MILLER AB Alias Summons awarde
-      commth. vs. George RODGERS AB same
pg 20
---- SamueL NEAL witeness-
-      commth vs. Robert HOLDERBY(Jr.) AB not guilty
-      commth vs. Thomas NEAL same
-      comth. vs Thomas CLAP same
-      commth vs. James WILKS AB caps awarded
-      commth vs. Samuel HUGGANS ab Alias Summons
-      commth.vs. James BYORS(Byers) AB caps awarded
-      commth vs. John HOLLANDBACK(Hollingback) AB not guilty and Cond
-      commth vs. Saml. FURGUSON AB Alias Summons
-      Daniel WITCHER Jr. witness
-      commth vs Johnaton BUFFINGTON show cause
-      (com. vs Patsy WHITECOTTON)
page 21------
-      Thomas EVANS and James LOCKHEART assee. of John WOODWARD
       vs. Henry HAMPTON, Henry BROWN, Reuben SLAUGHTER in debt
-      Thomas WARD vs. John HANNAN in case
-      commth. vs. George WARD indt. AB
-      same vs. Holly CRUMP indt. trespass
-      same vs. Peter COFFES (Coffee)indt. AB
-      same vs. James STEVENSON (Stephenson)
-      same vs. James POTEET
-      Mark RUSSELL & al(Henry HAYNIE,John RODGERS,Edmund MORRIS,[security
       for late sheriff Henry BROWN])vs. Thomas WARD
-      Andrew DONNALLY vs. Thomas WARD notice
page 22------
-      commth. vs. Thomas CLAP indt. AB not guilty
Jury : William D. MORRIS,William LOVE,James HOGAN, Henry HAMPTON, Benj.
BROWN,Joel ESTIS, Robert RUTHERFORD,William DUNBAR,John HARRIS, Daniel
FRANCE,John BURTON,Zachariah ESTILL. Def.guilty $5.00.

-      Phillip Fair (on demise of James MADISON vs. Jacob BACHGRAMBLE
       (BEECHGRIBBER) ejectment motion for John COX
-      Ammdab SEEKRIGHT vs. GARDNER & Co & DREADNOT (affadavits of Rich.
CRUMP coronor,Wit:David SPURLOCK,David HARBOUR,John LEE,Ezekiel
SLAUGHTER,tenants, Judgement for plf & possession given in ejectment
-      Manoah BOSTICK vs William MERRITT (& Mark RUSSELL) bond quashed
-      Commth vs Robert HOLDERBY jury same as above
page 23   7th may 1811 Tuesday   same judge
-      Commth vs Stephen KELLY discharged no jurisdiction

```
-------------
-    Thomas WARD vs John HANNAN(Charles ALSBURY,Wm.MORRIS)
Jury:William FULLERTON,John DAVIS,James HOGAN,James HOLDERBY,Mark
RUSSELL, John RODGERS, Richard SHARP, Edward PAULY,James HOSKINS, John
BLANKENSHIP,John MERRIT,William BUFFINGTON. FIND FOR PLF $16.66
-------------
-    (Andrew)DONNALLY(Clk of Kanawha Co.) vs (Thomas)WARD sheriff of
          Cabell Co. notice cont.
Wenesday  8TH MAY 1811   same judge-
-    Deed  of bargain between Chester HOW & wife(who reliquishes dower
          right)        to John LEE
-    Daniel RUFFNER vs John BARRETT(&Jno.REYNOLDS)  in debt & cont
-    (John)SIMMONS vs Wm.BUFFINGTON   CONT.
-    Ammadab SEEKRIGHT on demise of Chester HOW & wife(Nancy)
          vs Ferdinand DREADNOT ejectment  (by covt. with John LEE
-    plf by atty  vs John LEE  cont
-    Thomas BUFFINGTON Sr.vs William HOLDERBY Sr. in case-not guilty
-    Andrew DONNALLY vs Thomas WARD judgement $58.10
pg 25--------
-    commth vs Saml.SHORT  information $30
-    Thos.WARD vs HANNAN & al(ALSBURY & MORRIS)  in case $16.66
-    Thomas WARD & James HOLDERBY ordered to appear  gaming charge
8 may 1811
          "On the motion of the attorney for the Commonwealth and for the
reason appearing to the Court, it is agreed that Thomas WARD & James
HOLDERBY be severally summoned to appear forthwith before this court to
show cause why information should not be severally filed against them
and each of them for unlawful gaming at the Court House of the county of
Cabell being a place of publick resort during the last February term of
the said County Court in then and there playing at divers unlawful games
with cards and betting on the sides and hands of divers persons who then
and there were gaming and winning and lossing at those Games divers
large sums of money= and further that they the said Thomas WARD and
James HOLDERBY then being Justices of the Peace in the County of Cabell,
contary to the duties of their said offices did exhibit money for the
purpose of alluring persons to bet against and at unlawful games and the
monies then and there actully betted and stacked in their view, did not
siege and account as proscribed by the Several Acts of Assembly."
     (very few of the cases are 'so' recorded)
-    commth vs Thomas WARD  information filed
     "by affadvit-Horatio CATLETT -4 Jan 1811-contractor to carry
U.S.mail in Kanawha County to Millersburg,KY. He was stopped at mouth of
12 Pole by George WARD and Holly CRUMP who demanded his horse. WARD drew
a pistol which CATLETT thought was locked and repeated demand for horse
or be blown through. CRUMP took bridle of horse. Justice Henry HANEY
refused to issue warrants. WARD,CRUMP and HANEY ordered to appear to
answer inquiry."
-    same vs James HOLDERBY same
-    Alexander CATLETT Sr. vs James HOGAN  IN case
-    commth vs Thomas WARD  perjury (affadvits of Chester HOW,Thomas
BUFFINGTON Jr.,Edmund MORRIS,Esom HANNON,Thomas CLAP,William FULLERTON.
-    same vs HOLDERBY same-
pg 26    Thursday 1th may 1811  same Judge as yesterday
-    George DAVIDSON vs Brice STOKES  enq set aside plea not guilty
```

- same vs Pierson JOHNSTON same
- commth vs Thomas WARD gaming information filed
- commth vs James HOLDERBY same

Superior Court 2nd Monday after 4th Monday in Sept--7 oct 1811
Judge James ALLEN of 12th Circuit

-Grand Jury:Edmd.McGINNIS, James McGINNIS, William FULLERTON, John HATFIELD, Esom HANNAN, John MORRIS Sr., Thomas KILGORE, James JORDEN Sr, Joseph HILYARD, Lawrence BRYANT, William ADKINS, Hezekiah ADKINS, Berry ADKINS, John McMAHAN, Thomas BUFFINGTON Sr., Peter LOWER, Mark RUSSELL, John HARRISON, James SMITH & James HOLDERBY

pg 27---------
- fined for not atending Grand Jury: David HARBOUR, William JORDEN,
- Malchor STROOP, & Manoah BOSTICK
- (XX)Thomas WARD(XX)& Jack ESTIS -appear immediately
- Manoah BOSTICK vs William MERRITT (& Edmd.McGINNIS) bond-cont.

- Commth vs Jeremiah B.JACK larceny

jury:Daniel DOUTHAT,George DAVIDSON,Robt.WILSON,George HOLLANBACK,John MERRITT,John FERGUSON,Jacob HITE, William LOVE,Daniel WITCHER Sr., Robt. GOSDON,William WALKER, & Reuben BOOTON guilty 18 months in jail

Tuesday 8th Oct same judge
- Edward S.STRIBLING qualified atty

page 28 Grand Jury met as advertisement except John HARMON
indt.: Henry FRANCE AB
Littleberry ADKINS AB
James ADKINS AB
John LONG selling liquor without license
John SIMMONS nuisance
- Affidavits accepted: Jeffery RUSSELL,Mark RUSSELL,Edward CARDLE
- certificate of Reubon VAUGHN sent to Govenor
- Ammadab SEEKRIGHT on the demise of Chester HOW vs Martha SANDERS & John FORTH ejectment
- Ammadab SEEKRIGHT on demise of William HEPBURN & (John DUNDASS) vs William GREENWOOD,Wesly CORWELL,Charles CUMINGS & William ROSE (who are in possession) (affadvit of Burwell SPURLOCK) motion by Edmund MORRIS
- Ammadab SEEKRIGHT on demise of Chester HOW(and wife Nancy DUVALL) vs Ferdinando DREADNOT ejt.(atty Ballard SMITH) (affadvit by Burwell SPURLOCK saying John FORTH & Martha SANDERS are in possession of property)

Pg 29--------
- Commth vs Obadiah MERRITT

Jury:Henry HAYNIE,Moses McCOMAS,David McCOMAS,James WILSON,John BARRETT, Isom GARRETT,Spencer ELLIS,John FULLERTON,Stephen SPURLOCK,John AMOS, Henry PAYTON, & Jeffery RUSSELL. DEF GUILTY $1.00

- Andrew BARRETT,William DAVIS,Hugh MILLER,David DAVIS,George SPURLOCK fined for no appearance on petty Jury.-----
- commth vs Sanders WITCHER Indt Ab -witness James BYERS Sr.

- commth vs Daniel NEAL indt AB

Jury:Richard BROWN,Benjamin BROWN,Stephen BARTRAM,Robert REATHERFORD, Malchor STROOP,Samuel McGINNIS,Thomas CLAP,John MERRITT,Charles MOR-RISON, Daniel WITCHER Jr.,Daniel WITCHER Sr.,James MOMAN DEF Not guilty

```
-      Isaac RUSSELL, Stephen HENSLY, Pierson JOHNSON, fined no petty jury
-      commth vs Daniel WITCHER Jr. indt AB-witness called Daniel NEAL,
          Sampson SANDERS fined no appearance-ATTACHMENT
pg 30-------
-      commth vs John BYERS  def not guilty
-------------------
-      commth vs Charles STUART  indt AB
Jury:Henry HAYNIE, Andrew BARRETT, Moses McCOMAS, David McCOMAS, Henry
PAYTON, James WILSON, Hugh MILLER, John BARRETT, Daniel DAVIS, George
SPURLOCK, Isom GARRETT & Wm.BUFFINGTON
-------------------
-      commth vs Hugh MILLER indt AB not guilty
-      commth vs George RODGERS  indt AB caps awarde
-      commth vs Moses MOTT indt AB caps awd.
-------------------
-      commth vs Daniel NEAL indt AB
Jury:John RODGERS, Martin HOLLANDBACK, Richard BROWN, Robert WILSON, William
WALKER, John HOLLANDBACK, Wm.BARKER, Thomas CLAP, Lerose MERRITT, Stephen
BARTRAM, Stephen SPURLOCK, James GRAY  def not guilty
-------------------
-      commth vs (Samuel FERGUSON)
-      commth vs Saml. HUGGANS indt AB award
-      commth vs James BYERS indt AB caps awarded
-      commth vs John HOLLANDBACK  indt AB-
pg 31----------
-   Jury:Henry HAYNIE, Andrew BARRETT, Moses McCOMAS, David McCOMAS, James
WILSON, Hugh MILLER, John BARRETT, Daniel DAVIS, George SPURLOCK, Isom
GARRETT, & Wm.BUFFINGTON
-------------------
-      commth vs Jonathan BUFFINGTON fornication
-      same   vs Patsy WHITECOTTON same with above
-      commth vs George WARD indt AB cont
-      commth ve Peter COFFEE indt AB caps awarded
-      commth vs James STEPHENSON indt AB not guilty
-      commth vs James POTEET indt AB not guilty
-------------------
-      commth vs Thomas WARD informaton for gaming
Jury:George SPURLOCK, Henry HAYNIE, Moses McCOMAS, Danl.DAVIS, Isom
GARRETT, Stephen SPURLOCK, Malchor STROOP, Berry ADKINS, John RODGERS, Nath.
SCALES, William ADKINS & Jacob FUDGE
-------------------
-      Manoah BOSTICK vs William MERRITT cont
Court ajourned til tomorrow
pg 32          Wednesday 9 oct 1811  same judge
-      Sanders WITCHER vs Daniel WITCHER Sr. poss. of negroes
         (Wit: James BYORS & Mark RUSSELL for negro man HARRIS, girl PATSY,
          girl PHEBEY, boy DAVID, girl CHARLOTTE)
------------
-      commth vs James HOLDERBY information gaming
JURY:Hugh BOWEN, Jesse McCOMMAS, John BARRETT, Daniel WITCHER Sr., Thomas
CLAPP, Robert RUTHERFORD, Henry PEYTON, Joseph HILYARD, Saml.BENSON, Saml.
FERGUSON, John FERGUSON, John FULLERTON. def gulity $100 and his security
John RUSSELL $100
```

-     Henry HAMPTON Jr. vs James HOGAN debt
JURY:John FERGUSON,Hugha BOWEN,Jesse McCOMMAS,Henry PEYTON,Daniel
WITCHER Sr.,Josseph HILYARD,Saml.BENSON,James ALDRIDGE,John
FULLERTON,Achilles McGINNIS,Thomas CLAPP,Robert BUFFINGTON
def guilty costs $16.66

-     William DAVIS ,Daniel DAVIS,George SPURLOCK,Isaac RUSSELL,Pierson
JOHNSTON failed to attend jury

REVOLUTIONARY War service of Jeffery RUSSELL

"   The affidavitts of Jeffery RUSSELL, Mark RUSSELL, Edmund CREEDLE
were produced in the Court in the following words to wit: Jeffery
RUSSELL in open Court made oath on the holy Gosspels of God That about
the last of the year Seventeen hundred and seventy six in Meclenburg
County in the Commonwealth of Virginia as well as this affiant can now
recollect he enlisted for the term of three years and was placed in, as
a private, the fourthenth Regiment of the Virginia line on Continental
Establishment. That this affiant continued in the public service the
full term of three years and about the 28th of Demcember 1779 this
affiant was regularly discharged in the City of Philadelphia and
received a certificate there of from a Colonel left at that place for
the purpose of discharging those troops whose term of service had
expired, but whose name this affiant does not recollect. That this
affiant some years after his discharge, called at the office of the
auditor of the Public accounts of the Commonwealth of Virginia agreeable
to a general requisition for the officers and soliders of this state, to
bring in their respective claims, That he accepted his said discharge
given him signed by the Colonel above alluded to, in the auditors office
and rec'd a certificate for the compensation allowed by the Government
to the Soliders, for the depreciation of their pay. But this affiant not
being acquainted with the rules of office failed to receive a certified
copy of his discharge which was essential to this affiant receiving
regular evidence of the quantity of Land he was entitled to, according
to the terms of his enlistment and service, and this affiant further
states that the said certificate of discharge above alluded granted him
in Philadelphia as aforesaid and now in the office of the auditor of
Public accounts of this commonwealth contain the truth and was regularly
signed by the officer whose signature it bears, and that this affiant
hath never before proved or claimed his right to land for the service in
the said certificate of this discharge mentioned nor has he ever rec'd
any land or Land warrants for the said service, or in any manner
transfered his right to Land to any other person.
                                        Jeffery RUSSELL

     Mark RUSSELL made oath in open Court that he well recollects that
during the revolution War; the above named affiant Jeffery RUSSELL
enlisted into that part of the Army of the United States commonly called
the Virginia line on Continental establishment for the term of three
years, and that this affiant has seen the certificate of the Auditor of
Public accounts granted to the said Jeffery RUSSELL for his depreciation
of pay, and was well satisfied that the same was genuine-. That the
annexed certificate signed Reuben VAWGHN is in the hand writing and

signature of said VAUGHN. That at the date of said Certificate Mr.VAUGHN was a Justice of the peace for the County in said certificate mentioned, and had been a Captain of the Militia, and in the latter character was engaged in actual service in the revolutionary Ward.(War)
Mark RUSSELL

Edmund CREEDLE about forty five years of age, came before the Court and made oath, in due form of Law, saith that he lived in the neighbor-hood of Jeffery RUSSELL, at the time he enlisted into the public service in the course of the Revolutionary War that Mr.RUSSELL was generally understood and believed to have continued in that service for three years and to have been regularly discharged.
Edmund CREEDLE

Oct.ther 2d.1784 Mecklinburg County Virginia, This is to certify that Jeffery RUSSELL who is about to remove out of the state into the North State, is a man that was born and raised in the settlement and neighborhood from whence he is now about to go from, and this is certifying this said Jeffery RUSSELL is a man that I had been intimately acquainted with from his infant days and I further asscert that he has ever been under the character of an honest industrious quiet peacable person and has served four years truly and honestly in the contest between Britten and America, and has ever had an unspoted character, by both oficers and man. Given under our hands.
Reuben VAUGHN
Sworn to and ordered to be certified to the Executive of the Comm'th of Virginia. "

pg 33--------
- Henry HAMPTON vs James HOGAN   plea not guilty
- Thomas WARD   vs Manoah BOSTICK   case
- Richard BROWN vs Thomas WARD in case writ of inquiry

- George DAVIDSON vs Brice STOKES in case
Jury:Robert REATHERFORD,Joseph HILYARD,Henry PEYTON,Achilles McGINNIS, John FULLERTON,Daniel WITCHER Sr.,Zachariah T.ESTILL,James ALDRIDGE,Jesse McCOMAS,Chester HOW,Hugh BOWEN,Saml.BENSON find for plf
----
- Manoah BOSTICK vs William MERRITT & al(Edmd.McGINNIS)   notice cond
pg 34 ------Tuesday 10th oct 1811   same Judge
- commth vs Jeremiah B.JACKSON guilty confined 1/3 his time in cells
- Fredrick HAMNIER(Hammer) vs Nathaniel SCALES,Robert ADAMS,Noah SCALES debt   of $330.25 & 6 % from 16 jun 1804

- Danl.RUFFNER(assee of Joseph RUFFNER decd and his exec.John REYNOLDS   vs John BARRETT in debt
Jury:Joseph HILYARD,Mark RUSSELL,Danl. WITCHER Sr.,James HOLDERBY, Zachariah T.ESTILL,Robert REATHERFORD,Obadiah MERRITT,Saml.SHORT,Henry PAYTON,William T.CROSS,Reuben SLAUGHTER, Lerose MERRITT
pg 35--------
- Manoah BOSTICK vs William MERRITT(Edmd.McGINNIS)judt/ obligation
- Thomas BUFFINGTON Sr. vs William HOLDERBY Sr.
- (Jeremiah B.JACKSON(late of Cabell)convicted of larceny to be imprisoned in publick jail & penitentary for 18 months in solitary cell)
- (commth vs Samuel NEAL attachment)

```
-       (commth vs Daniel WITCHER attachment)
------------------
-       George DAVIDSON vs Pearson JOHNSON
Jury:Peter SCALES,Benjamin BROWN,Charles STUART,Christian YOUST,James
HOLDERBY,Samuel SHORT,Larose MERRITT,Alexander CATLETT,James RHEI,
Reuben SLAUGHTER,George DAVISON,William FULLERTON fined plf $60 dam
------------------
-       Horatio CATLETT vs Holly CRUMP (& George WARD) trespass
pg 36-----------
-       Mark RUSSELL orders himself  Spc  B  - court adjourned
Friday 11th oct 1811   same judge
-       Daniel RUFFNER assee vs John BARRETT in debt-agnt John HANEY(Henry)
-       commth vs George WARD & H.CRUMP informationn
-       commth vs H.HANEY (Haynie) information
-       H.CATLETT vs G.WARD  & al TRESPASS -George DAVIS cost
-       Horatio CATLETT bond $200 to give evidence for G.WARD & H.EVANS(?)
pg 37-----------
-       commth vs Thomas WARD & James HOLDERBY  malfeziance in office
-       commth vs HOLDERBY & al attachment & costs
-       commth vs Thomas WARD  rule for perjury-information filed
-       Kennth BLAKE vs Henry HAYNIE  AB  security required
-       John SIMMONS vs William BUFFINGTON writ awarded to establish ferry
pg 38-----------
-       Ammadab SEEKRIGHT for William HEPBURN & John DUNDASS (atty PRESTON)
        vs Ferdinando DREADNOT-John EVERETT & William GREENWOOD def-instead
-       Ammadab SEEKRIGHT on the demise of Chester HOWE & wife (Nancy)
          vs Ferdinando DREADNOT by Martha SANDERS (atty Thos.L.PRESTON)
          (6 massuages,4 cottages,1/6 OF 1000a of DIAMOND SURVEY)
-       Noah SCALES  & al(Edmd.MORRIS,Rich.CRUMP,Elisha McCOMAS-Trustees of
Guyandotte) vs Daniel WITCHERS Sr. & al(Nathaniel SCALES)
          -Mark RUSSELL special bail
-       Noah SCALES & al  (see trustees above) vs
        John SIMMONS & Daniel DAVIS-- John RODGERS justified payment
-       Jailor(Robt.HOLDERBY)       $15
-       Clerk (Edmd.MORRIS)         $15       James WILSON  prosecutor 5 days-
-       sheriff(Jesse SPURLOCK)     $10
Pg 39-----------
   Superior Court 2nd Monday after 4th Monday in Apr. --11 may 1812
                Judge James ALLEN  of the 12 Circuit Court
-       Henry WHITE   qualified atty
-       Andrew HAZE      "       atty(Hays)
-----------
-Grand Jury: Mark RUSSELL,Manoah BOSTICK,Elisha McCOMAS,William
BUFFINGTON, Benjamin BROWN,Edmund McGINNIS,Samuel SMILEY,John RODGERS,
George RODGERS,David SPURLOCK,George SPURLOCK,Wm.ADKINS,James BYERS,
James HOLDERBY,Isom GARRETT,Joseph GARRETT,Hezekiah ADKINS,Thomas CLAP,
John McMAHAN.  returns:
-----------
-       Manoah BOSTICK vs Thomas WARD & John RUSSELL special bail Gilbert
          STEPHENSON, Edmund MORRIS
-       Amamdab SEEKRIGHT on demise of HEPBURN & DUNDASS  vs John EVERETT
page 40----------
-       Lawrence BRYANT,Stephen KELLY,Noah SCALES,John WARD,John LONG
          fined for not attending Grand Jury $8
```

```
-----------
-      commth vs Sanders WITCHER   AB
Jury:John MORRIS Jr., Henry HAYNIE, Richard BROWN, Charles BOOTHE, John
FERGUSON, John HOLLANDBACK, Benjamin DAVIS, James GRAY, Wm. CLARK, Daniel
FRANCE, Jeffery RUSSELL & William JORDEN   verdict for def
-----------
-      Amamdab SEEKRIGHT demise of Wm.HEPBURN, L.DUNDASS
           vs Edmund MORRIS
-----------
-      commth vs Daniel WITCHER, Jr.
Jury:Jacob HITE, Wm.MERRITT, Gilbert SULLIVAN, Daniel DOUTHAT, John BARRETT,
Noah SCALES, Wm.T.CROSS, Lawrence BRYANT, Wm.THOMPSON, John GRIFFITH,
Zachariah T.ESTILL, John HATFIELD def guilty fine $5
pg 41---------
-      William CHANDLER vs Wm.MORRISON
-      William CHANDLER vs Sanders WITCHER(&Daniel WITCHER Jr. & William
           MORRISON) AB
-      Richard CRUMP vs Daniel MORGAN (Charles MORGAN exec of Simon MORGAN
           decd) case
-      Rule vs Hugh BOWEN information & cause commth vs BYORS
-      commth vs George RODGERS indt AB   no guilty
pg 42---------
-      commth vs Hugh MILLER
Jury:John MORRIS Jr., Henry HAYNIE, Richard BROWN, Charles BOOTH, John
FERGUSON, John HOLLANDBACK, Benjamin DAVIS, James GRAY, Wm.CLARK, Daniel
FRANCE, Jeffery RUSSELL & Wm.JORDAN   guilty $5
-----------
-      commth vs George RODGERS indt AB
-      commth vs James BYERS  indt AB plea not guilty
-      commth vs Moses MOTT  indt AB  caps awarded
-      Commth vs James WILKS  indt AB  caps awarded
-      commth vs Saml.HUGGANS(Huggins)  indt AB caps awarded
pg 43------------
-      commth vs Saml.FERGUSON  indt AB
-      commth vs P.COFFEE  Indt AB  n.g. & cont.
------------------
-      commth vs James HENDERSON(Stephenson ?)    indt AB
Jury:Henry HAYNIE, Rich.BROWN, Chas.BOOTH, John FERGUSON, John HOLLENBACK,
Benj.DAVIS, James GRAY, Wm.CLARK, Daniel FRANCE, Jeffery RUSSELL, Wm.JORDEN,
& Henry HATCHER    Guilty $10
-----------
-      commth vs James POTEET  indt AB
-      commth vs George WARD
-      commth vs Henry FRANCE   indt AB
-      same   vs Littleberry ADKINS  indt AB
-      Manoah BOSTICK & Daniel HARBER excused as Grand Jurors
-      Daniel NEAL  bond $50 summoned to appear tomorrow
page 44---------
     Tuesday 12th May 1812 same Judge as yesterday
Grand Jury met and adjourned
     William JORDEN excused as Grand Juror
-----------
-      commth vs John MORRIS Jr.  indt-plea not guilty
```

Jury:Jesse McCOMAS,Henry HAYNIE,Leonard SWEARINGIN,Charles BOOTH, John
EVERETT,Holly CRUMP,Gilbert STEPHENSON, Newton GARDNER,Jacob FUDGE,
Robert WILSON,Benj.STEPHENSON & John HATFIELD deft fined $16

-Grand Jury indt: Jno.STUART   AB indt
                  Isaac CONLEY   AB indt
                  John WARD   unlawful gaming
                  Chester HOW   same
                  Edward RHEA   same
                  Obadiah MERRITT   same
                  James TURLEY   same
                  John BURCHAM   same
                  Daniel WITCHER Jr. same
                  John MERRITT Sr. same
                  Hugh BOWEN   same
pg 45----------
-    Manoah BOSTICK vs Sampson SAUNDERS   IN CASE found for plf costs
-summons issued for all indt of Grand Jury
-    Sampson SAUNDERS fined for not appearing as witness-dismissed
----

    on testimony of Wm.DUNBARE it appears supb. against John MORRIS 18th
Feb that Simmon M.WOOD gave false info. Hugh BOWEN deputy sheriff
summoned to appear
pg 46--------
-    John LONG fined for not appearing as witness-dismissed
-    Stephen KELLY fined not appearing as Grand Juror-excused
-.   (Daniel DAVIS same)
-    Manoah BOSTICK vs Thomas WARD & al(& John RUSSELL) in debt
         Jesse SPURLOCK witness
-    (Commth vs Henry FRANCE AB)
-    (Hugh BOWEN deputy sheriff for Jesse SPURLOCK sheriff)
-.   (James BYERS contempt)
 Wednesday 13th may 1812 same judge as yesterday

-    commth vs George WARD indt AB
Jury:Robert SLAUGHTER,Goodrich SLAUGHTER,John BARRETT,Samuel SMILEY,
John EVERETT,John HATFIELD,Jesse McCOMAS,Thos.CLAP,James HOLDERBY,
William WALKER,William BRUMFIELD,Perry JOHNSON guilty fine $43
pg 47---------
-    commth vs POTEET indt AB
-    commth vs George WARD (& Holly CRUMP)Information & cont.

-    commth vs Thomas WARD info for gaming
Jury:Holly CRUMP,Israel HEATH,William THOMPSON,Isaac BOULT,William
BUFFINGTON,Charles BOOTH,John JONES,Elisha McCOMAS,Joseph HILYARD,
Jeffery RUSSELL,William HOLDERBY, Reuben CRAWFORD Def guilty

-    commth vs David NEAL ATTACHMENT for contempt(as wit: against Danl.
         WITCHER Jr.
-    Noah SCALES & al vs John SIMMONS & al   in debt
pg 48--------
-    Noah SCALES & al vs Danl.WITCHER & al in debt
-    (Philip)FAIRPLAY on demise of James MADISON vs John COX in ejt
-    (SEEKRIGHT) on demise of C.HOWE & al(wife Nancy) vs M.SAUNDERS ejt

- HEPBURN & DUNDASS vs John EVERETT & al (Wm.GREENWOOD)in ejectment
    Edmd.MORRIS,Jeremiah WARD,WM.GREENWOOD- witnesses-(LAND PATENTED
in name of Zachariah T.ESTILL & Edmd.MORRIS)
- same vs Edmd.MORRIS EJECTMENT(land patented in name of Joseph
CHILDERS and William MORRIS includes 2nd falls of Mud River)
- John SIMMONS vs W.BUFFINGTON on appeal for ferry
pg 49---------
- commth & John MORRIS Jr. vs Thomas WARD execution quashed

- John HIGHZY vs James MOMAN AB
Jury:Elisha McCOMAS,Reuben CRAWFORD,Israel HEATH,William THOMPSON,
Charles BOOTHE,Isaac BOULT,John JONES,William HOLDERBY,Stephen WILSON,
Jeffery RUSSELL,William BUFFINGTON,& Joseph HEILY

- Thomas WARD vs Manoah BOSTICK plea not guilty
Jury:Wm.BRUMFIELD,Richard CRUMP,George ROGERS,Wm.WALKER,James HOLDERBY,
John EVERETT,Robert HOLDERBY,John HATFIELD,Samuel SMILEY,Goodrich
SLAUGHTER,Robert SLAUGHTER, Thomas CLAP. verdict for def

- trustees of Guyandotte(Noah SCALES,Edmund MORRIS,Richard
CRUMP,Elisha McCOMAS,(& Henry BROWN decd) vs John SIMMONS &Danl.DAVIS
- trustees of Guyandotte vs Daniel WITCHER Sr. & Nathaniel SCALES
page 50-------- Thursday 14th May 1812 same judge
- Adam DICKISON(DICKERSON)assee vs David Spurlock inf debt
    witness Edmund McGINNIS & Squire TONEY
- commth vs Chester HOWE unlawful gaming ng & cont
- Daniel WITCHER Jr. vs Chester HOWE & al(wife Nancy) in case
    William SPURLOCK special bond

- Daniel RUFFNER assee vs John BARRETT
Jury:John EVERRETT,Manoah BOSTICK,John GRIFFITH,Noah SCALES, Henry
HAYNIE,John LONG,Henry TUNKLE(yes),Charles BOOTH,Daniel DOUTHAT, Sampson
SANDERS,Joseph HILYARD & Daniel WITCHER Jr. (often verdict is no given)
page 51----------
- commth vs Thomas WARD information on gaming
- WARD & John RODGERS fined $100
- SEEKRIGHT &Chester HOWE &(wife Nancy) vs David SPURLOCK ejt cont
----
- commth & John MORRIS Jr. vs Thomas WARD(Sheriffs bond by Jeremiah
WARD,Noah SCALES,Manoah BOSTICK. Wit:Edmd.MORRIS,Henry BROWN)
Jury:xxChester HOWExx,Charles BOOTH,Sampson SANDERS,Squire TONEY,Daniel
DOUTHAT,Elisha McCOMAS,John GRIFFITH,John LONG,John EVERETT,Henry
HAYNIE,Richard CRUMP,John HATFIELD,& James McGINNIS

- commth vs Thomas WARD(as sheriff) perjury   def costs
page 52---------
- commth vs James HOLDERBY Contempt--discharged costs
- Horatio CATLETT vs George WARD AB awarded
- COMMTH vs Samuel NEAL contempt costs

- Richard BROWN vs Thos.WARD
Jury:James HOLDERBY,Holly CRUMP,Jacob FUDGE,Robert HOLDERBY,William
BUFFINGTON,Philip RUSSELL,Chester HOWE,David SPURLOCK,William CLARK,
Samuel SMILEY,John FURGUSON,James GRAY for plf $60

page 53----------
- Henry HAMPTON vs James HOGAN judgement
- Sanders WITCHER vs Daniel WITCHER Sr.
  Friday May 15th 1812 same judge as yesterday
- Alex.CATLETT Sr.vs John McMAHAN case James HOLDERBY surety/costs
- Wm.HOLDERBY vs John SIMMONS cont
- John McMAHAN vs Jesse SPURLOCK &al(Alex.CATLETT) case
- Frederick HAMMER vs John SIMMONS debt
page 54--------
- John WILSON vs John McMAHAN set aside
- Daniel WITCHER Sr. vs Daniel WITCHER Jr. AB set aside
- Wm.CHANDLER vs Sanders WITCHER & al(Danl.WITCHER Jr.&Wm.MORRISON)
  set aside/cont.
- commth vs J.BYERS alias attachment awarded

- commth vs John WARD unlawful gaming
Jury:John HATFIELD,Holly CRUMP,Daniel DOUTHATT,Chester HOW,Henry HAYNIE,
John FERGUSON,John SIMMONS,Wm.WALKER,Richd. CRUMP,Wm.RUSSELL,Phillip
RUSSELL,Wm.CLARK def guilty

- commth vs Daniel WITCHER Jr. gaming
page 55----------
- Daniel WITCHER Jr. & his surety Chester HOWE $50 each-bond
- clk- $15.00
- Sheriff   10.00
- Jailor   15.00
- atty for commth $25 for 5 days
- commth vs John MERRITT gaming/cont.-----------
[Information in the first Law Order Book 1809-1812 ends at this
point and is picked up in Law Order Book 1812-1815.]
END Book I-(begin LO book 1812-1819)
page 56------------------------
   Superior Court of Law 12th oct 1812-James ALLEN Judge
-Grand Jury:Benjamin BROWN,Henry HATCHER,Robert CASEBOLT,John GRIFFITH,
William McCOMAS,Ransom DIAL,William ADKINS,Thomas WARD,John MORRIS,
Patten WALKER,Esom HANNAN,Robert WILSON,James SMITH,Samuel
STEPHENSON,Andrew BARRETT,Moses McCOMAS & James HOLDERBY

- Nathan SCALES finded for not attending Grand Jury
- Commth vs Benjamin GARRETT gaming/writ of error
- commth vs James TURLEY gaming-surety Danl.WITCHER $100
page 57----------
- commth vs John WARD gaming -discharged on his recog.fine $100
  sureties of $500 - to be delivered to the overseers of the poor
  and hired out for one month-surety John WARD & Thomas WARD
- Noah SCALES & al(LO-Edmd.MORRIS,Rich.CRUMP,Elisha McCOMAS)
  vs John SIMMONS & al(LO-Daniel DAVIS,William SPURLOCK,Henry
  HAYNIE) -forth coming bond
- Herbert P.GAINES amitted atty(LO)
- Grand Jury indt.:Richard W.EVANS-murder
            Benjamin GARRET Jr. gaming(LO)
            William RUSSELL gaming(LO)
- Daniel RUFFNER assee vs John BARRETT & al(LO & Edward BARRETT
  /forth coming bond

```
-      summons issued against Peter DIRTING, jailor to show cause why he
          allowed Beal KELLY to escape
page 58-----------
-Grand Jury indt.: Beal KELLY-larceny,
                   Jesse BLANKENSHIP AB
----------
-      Commth vs John BYERS AB
Jury:John WELLMAN,William DEMSEY,William JORDEN,Daniel WALKER,Thomas
VAUGHN,Kenneth BLAKE,Thomas CLAP,Isom GARRETT,William GREENWOOD,Isaac
CONLEY,Jacob FUDGE,Samuel SMILEY, Not guilty
-----------
-      commth vs Beal KELLY larceny
Jury:John RODGERS,Jesse SPURLOCK,Abijah SPERRY,John BARRETT,Mathew
PETERS,James TURLEY,John WELLMAN,Thos.VAUGHN,Thos.CLAP,Isom
GARRETT,James BOULT,Danl.WALKER not guilty
-----------
-      John HOLLANBACK & Henry HAMPTON fined-------court adjourned
page 59 ------- Tuesday 13th oct 1812  same judge
-      commth vs Moses MOTT assualt
-      commth vs James WILKS AB
-      commth vs Saml.FERGUSON AB
-        "    vs Saml.HUGGANS  AB(LO)
-------------
-      commth vs Peter COFFEE AB
Jury:William SPURLOCK,James BOLT,Jesse SPURLOCK,John WELMAN,Samuel
SMILEY,William McCOMAS,Daniel WITCHER,Abijah SPERRY,Peter LOWER, Micager
FRAZER,Andrew BARRETT & Samuel STEPHENSON guilty $5
Pg 60-------
-      commth vs Jasmes POTEET  AB
Jury:John BARRETT,Matthew PETERS,James BYERS,William FULLERTON,John
GRIFFITH,Isaac CONLEY,John MERRITT,Samuel NEAL,Esom
HANNAN,Jas.TURLEY,John HIGHZY,Henry HAYNIE not guilty
-----------
-      commth vs Thos.WARD information as justice of peace -plea & cont.
-      commth vs James HOLDERBY same
-      Commth vs Henry FRANCE AB
-      commth vs Littleberry ADKINS AB    Jury:same as above  not guilty
-      commth vs Thomas WARD Perjury
-        "    vs James ADKINS  AB(LO)
-        "    vs John STUART   trespass(LO)
-        "    vs Isaac CONLEY  AB(LO)
-      Adam DICKINSON assee of Thomas EVANS vs David SPURLOCK jud.$200(LO)
------------------
-      commth vs Chester HOW  gaming(LO)
Jury:John WELLMAN,Jesse SPURLOCK,Andrew BARRETT,Peter LORE,Hezekiah
ADKINS,John MORRIS Jr.,John AMOS,Esom HANNAN,Jacob FUDGE,William
MERRITT,James MAYO,David McCOMAS guilty $20 & costs
------------------
-      commth vs Edward REA        gaming(LO)
-        "    vs Obadiah MERRITT gaming(LO)
-        "    vs John MERRITT    gaming(LO)
-        "    vs Hugh BOWEN      gaming(LO)
no 61/62 just misnumbered not missing
page 63----------
```

- commth vs Daniel WITCHER Jr. gaming- not guilty
    NOTE:same jury as for Chester HOWE
- commth vs John BURCHIM Gaming-(same jury as above) guilty
- Daniel WITCHER Sr. vs Daniel WITCHER Jr.. AB(dismissed by plf)
- William MERRITT vs Edmund McGINNIS motion to establish ferry
- MADISON heirs vs John COX ejectment
- Chester HOWE & ua vs David SPURLOCK ejectment
Court adjourned
page 64----------
- (LO-Amamdab SEEKRIGHT demise of William)HEPBURN &(John) DUNDASS plf
    vs John EVERETT def-ejectment
- Noah SCALES grand jury indt excused
- C.R.MANAZOR plf vs William MERRITT & al(LO-William HOLDERBY Sr.
- Daniel WITCHER Sr. ball payment-judgement set aside
- Daniel HENSLEY vs John SIMMONS & al(James WILSON,& Bird LOCKHEART
    debt--Saml.SHORT special bail

- commth vs Daniel WITCHER Jr. gaming
Jury:James HOLDERBY,Elisha McCOMAS,William McCOMAS,Matthew PETERS,Hugh
MILLER,Samuel SMILEY,John MORRIS Jr.,Melchor STROOP,William SPURLOCK,
Henry HATCHER,Henry HAYNIE, & Robert HOLDERBY   not guilty
pg 65-----------
- commth vs John MERRITT gaming/jury same guilty $100-J.RUSSELL sec
- Edmund McGINNIS vs Samuel NEAL case dis. by plf
- same vs John A.BURCHAM same
- Thomas BUFFINGTON Sr. vs William HOLDERbx on appeal
- Holderby vs Buffington see above
- commth vs Daniel WITCHER Jr. an attachment
- Manoah BOSTICK assee of(LO-Wm.SKINNER & Levi BARBER)
    vs Thomas WARD & al(LO-John RUSSELL)
pg 66------------
- commth vs Hugh BOWEN gaming jury same as above-guilty fine $100
    recog.John RUSSELL
- commth vs John MORRIS Jr. vs Thomas WARD debt-cont
- commth vs John WARD gaming
- James WILSON vs John McMAHAN trespass
- Hugh CAPERTON vs Henry TURLEY jury same as above(21 pounds & ints)
page 67----------
- Frederick HAMNER vs John SIMMONS debt
- William HOLDERBY Sr. vs John SIMMONS case (death of Plantiff ?)
- John McMAHAN vs Jesse SPURLOCK &(LO-Alex.CATLETT) trespass cont
- George HAIRSTON vs Saml. SHELTON debt
- Daniel WITCHER Jr. vs Chester HOW &(LO wife)case dis.set aside
- commth vs Hugh BOWEN rule-payment of costs
- commth vs Jesse SPURLOCK rule (3 cases)
page 68-----------
- Edmund McGINNIS vs David CARTMILL case-deposition of Jeremiah WARD
- John McMAHAN   vs A.CATLETT Jr.case
- commth   vs Peter DIRTING rule
- commth   vs Robert HOLDERBY jallor account $35.00
    #2 $24.82, #3 $2.20
page 69-----------
- John JACKSON assee of(LO-Bird LOCKHEART)
    vs John SIMMONS &(LO-John WILSON) -Samuel SHORT special bail

```
-.        (Robert HOLDERBY jailor account $24.82)
  Thursday      15th oct 1812     same judge
-      John CHAMBERS account certified for guarding jail $35
-      Edmund MORRIS same
-      James WILSON allowed 4 days
-      Peter DIRTING jailor account
-      Peter DIRTING jailor & his surety:Wm.MERRITT,Larose MERRITT,
          Benjamin DAVIS gave bond
-      Samuel SHORT sheriff $15(LO)
-      (commth vs Thos.WARD perjury
page 70 -------   Superior Court 10th May 1813 Judge James ALLEN
-GRAND JURY:James HOLDERBY,William SPURLOCK,Samuel SMILEY,Jacob FUDGE,
William HOLDERBY,Richard CRUMP,John McMAHAN,Isom GARRETT,Stephen BEAN,
William FURGUSON,Moses McCOMAS,Elisha McCOMAS,Daniel DAVIS,Sanders
WITCHER,Thomas CLAP,James MAYO, & Berry BROWN.  indt.
------------
-      XX Stephen KELLY & William HAMPTON XX
-      Micajah BRUMFIELD indt AB
page 71   ----------
-      Stephen KELLY,William HAMPTON,John MORRIS Jr.,John WELLMAN &
Abraham SYORUS--- summons issued
-      Henry HAYNIE vs Horatio CATLETT & Sanders WITCHER Bond
          judgement against WITCHER
-      Frederick HAMMER vs Noah SCALES & others(LO-David McCOMAS, William
          BRUMFIELD) notice proved on bond
-      Ammadab SEEKRIGHT ON DEMISE OF Moses McCORMACK(LO-James,Richard,
          Sarah & Joshua McCOMAS) vs Ferdinando DREADNOT   ejectment
          Elizabeth MORGAN & Daniel MORGAN made deft-surety ordered
          (LO-500A & 5 houses atty David CARTMILL)
------------
-      commth vs Samuel FERGUSON indt AB
Jury:Jesse BLANKENSHIP,Charles CUMINGS,John GRIFFITH,Daniel WITCHER,
Kenneth BLAKE,Thomas BUFFINGTON,Daniel WALKER,William FULLERTON,Charles
STUART,Sampson SANDERS,William McCOMAS,Daniel MORGAN not guilty
page 72------------
-      William CHANDLER vs William MORRISON AB dismissed
-      William CHANDLER vs Daniel WITCHER Jr.& others(LO-Sanders WITCHER &
          William MORRISON) AB dismissed
-      commth vs James WILKS AB
-      commth vs Samuel HUGGANS  AB
--------------
-   commth vs Thomas WARD   malf.in office
Jury:Paul DAVIS,George RODGERS,Henry HAYNIE,Joseph BARRETT,John
HATFIELD, John BURTON,Andrew BARRETT,Samuel BARRETT,Nathaniel
SCALES,Jesse McCOMAS,William WALKER,William SPURLOCK  not guilty
page 73------------
-      Nathaniel SCALES fined & discharged not on Grand Jury
-      Ammadab SEEKRIGHT on demise of James WATSON   [[GRANT]]
          (for 5000a arable land and 72,202a woodland)
              vs Ferdinando DREADNOT,Edmund McGINNIS,William HAMPTON,Robert
REATHERFORD,Asa HATTON,William WALKER,Paul DAVIS,Thomas WARD,Joseph
GARRETT order of survey-wit Hugh BOWEN  possession to plf
------------
-      commth vs James HOLDERBY malf.as justice
```

-     commth vs John STUART AB
Jury:James SMITH,John EVERETT Jr.,John CAMPBELL,Sanders WITCHER,Patten WALKER,William BRUMFIELD,James MAYO,John McMAHAN,James TURLEY,Daniel WITCHER Sr.,Thomas BUFFINGTON Sr.& William HOLDERBY guilty
page 74-----------
-     commth vs Henry FRANCE AB
-     (Alex,) CATLETT & (Joseph)GARNER vs John McMAHAN securety $200

-     commth vs Isaac CONLEY AB
Jury:Samuel SMILEY,James GRAY,Sampson SANDERS,Daniel WITCHER Jr.,
William FULLERTON,Andrew BARRETT,Samuel BARRETT,Saml. FERGUSON,Henry HAYNIE,William SPURLOCK,William WALTON,George DENISON guilty
----
-     commth vs Edward REA gaming(LO-RAY)
-     commth vs Obadiah MERRITT gaming
page 75-----------
-     Joshua JONES vs George RODGERS covenant
        William MERRITT security - Elisha McCOMAS special bail
----
-     commth vs James BRYAN(LO-BYERS) AB
Jury:Samuel SMILEY,Sampson SANDERS,Daniel WITCHER Jr.,William FULLERTON,
Andrew BARRETT,Samuel BARRETT,Samuel FERGUSON,Henry HAYNIE,William
SPURLOCK,William WALTON,George DENISON,Daniel WALKER guilty

-     Greenberry KELLY vs Kenneth BLAKE Trespass
-     John SAMUELS qualifies as atty
-     William HAMPTON deliquent juror
-     commth vs John HOLLANDBACK fined not appearing witness
-     same   vs Henry HAMPTON same
page 76 --------   11th may 1813 same judge
-     John McMAHAN   vs Alexander CATLETT case
-     commth & John MORRIS vs Thos.WARD debt
-     James HOLDERBY adm/estate of William HOLDERBY
        vs John SIMMONS dismissed
-     C.(Claudius)B.MENAGER   vs William MERRITT & William HOLDEBY debt
Jury:Samuel SMILEY,John HATFIELD,Sanders WITCHER,Thos.CLAP,John
FERGUSON,John RODGERS,James POTEET,Wm.HAYNIE,Charles STUART,Daniel
MORGAN,Wm.McCOMAS,Alex.CATLETT Jr. fine interest to be paid from 1811

-     Manoah BOSTICK assee/(LO-William SKINNER & Levi BARBOUR)
        vs Thos.WARD & Jno.RUSSELL
Jury: same + Wm.BRUMFIELD(instead of Witcher) debt $.01
-     John JACKSON(LO assee/ Byrd LOCKHEART) vs John SIMMONS(& James
WILSON) debt Jury: same with Witcher $63.51 + interest from 180
-     David HENSLEY vs John SIMMONS,Byrd LOCKHEART, & James WILSON
        (trading under the name of John Simmons & Co.)
Jury:same $317.78 + 6% interest from 1809
page 79-----------
-     commth vs Thomas WARD perjury
Jury:Stephen BEAN,Charles RAMSEY,William CLARK,James WILSON,William
HAYNIE,Daniel MORGAN,Thos.HATFIELD,William McCOMAS,Thomas BUFFINGTON Sr.
James POTEET,John SIMMONS,John HOLLANDBACK guilty fine $10

-     Richard CRUMP sworn to attend above jury

```
               11th may 1813  same judge
-      John McMAHAN vs Jesse SPURLOCK & Alexander CATLETT Jr. tres/dis
-      Edmund MORRIS -clk,Peter DINGESS-jailor,Samuel SHORT-sheriff
       James WILSON-PA
page 80---------
-      Thomas WARD bond $100 with Mark RUSSELL,Henry HAYNIE,& James WILSON
his security at $333.33 each- Ward to appear tomorrow & not depart
without leave of court
-      commth vs George WARD (LO & Holly CRUMP)  information for trespass
------------
-      James WILSON vs John McMAHAN  trespass
Jury:William WALKER,William HAYNIE,Daniel WITCHER Sr.Sanders WITCHER,
Jesse SPURLOCK,Thomas CLAP,John FERGUSON,Daniel MORGAN,William MERRITT,
Thomas BUFFINGTON Sr.,Daniel WALKER, William McCOMAS  $70 + interest
------------
-      Horatio CATLETT vs George WARD (LO & Holly CRUMP) debt
page 81-----------
-      Greenberry KELLY vs Kenneth BLAKE- Stephen KELLY for costs
-      Stephen KELLY excused from Grand Jury
-      A.CATLETT Sr. vs John McMAHAN trespass- not guilty
-      George DENISON (LO & Mark RUSSELL) vs John ARMSTRONG case  dism.
-      Mark RUSSELL vs Henry HAMPTON debt- special bail Richd. CRUMP
-      Robert DOUTHAT vs Henry HAMPTON debt-special bail Richd.CRUMP
-      Edmd.McGINNIS vs David CARTMILL case
-      Richd.SHARP vs Stephen KELLY
page 82----------
-      William WALKER vs James BARRETT case  dism.
-      Thomas BUFFINGTON vs James HOLDERBY (LO-adm/Wm.HOLDERBY Sr.dec)
-      George DAVIDSON vs Pierson JOHNSON case
-      James HOLDERBY adm. vs William BUFFINGTON dismissed
-      (LO-Wm.MERRITT vs Edmund McGINNIS establish ferry across Ohio)
page 83--------      Thursday 13th may 1813  same judge
-      George HAIRSTON vs Samuel SHELTON debt
-      commth vs Thomas WARD information for perjury
         (LO-security Mark RUSSELL,Henry HAYNIE,James WILSON)
page 84-----Superior Court Cabell County 11th Oct 1813-Judge James ALLEN
-      Manoah BOSTICK vs Thomas WARD & Wm.BRUMFIELD bond
-Grand Jury:Edmund McGINNIS,Benjamin BROWN,James MAYO,Sampson SANDERS,
Lawrence BRYANT,Jacob FUDGE,Patten WALKER,John EVERETT Sr.,Noah SCALES,
Sanders WITCHER,John HATFIELD,William D.MORRIS,George RODGERS,Samuel
FERGUSON,William WALTEN,Isaac McCOMAS,Charles BOOTH,William FERGUSON,
John BURTON,James SNODGRASS,John WALLACE,James HOLDERBY,Adam HATFIELD
------------
-      John MORRIS Jr. & John WELLMAN excused from Grand Jury
-      Abraham SYRES same
page 85--------
-      commth vs James WILKS  AB
-      same    vs Saml. HUGGANS  AB
-      commth vs Chester HOWE  gaming
-      commth vs John BURCHAM  gaming
-      commth vs Micajah FRAZURE  AB (LO-BRUMFIELD not Frazure))
-      commth vs Richard W.EVANS  murder
-      commth vs Henry FRANCE  AB
page 86-----------
```

-Jury:William HATFIELD,Phillip BUMGARDNER,Daniel WITCHER Jr.,William
MERRITT,John CAMPBELL,John EVERETT Jr.,Gilbert STEPHENSON,Samuel
McGINNIS,Abraham SIRES,James POTEET,& William HATFIELD guilty
James MOMAN the prosecutor

-      commth vs James ADKINS   AB

-      commth vs Edward REA gaming
Jury:James McGINNIS,John HANAN,John MORRIS Jr.,John HOLLANDBACK, Leonard
SHARP,Wm.HAMPTON,Charles RAMSEY,Abraham SYRUS,William HATFIELD,James
MOMAN,Samul. McGINNIS & William MERRETT guilty

-      commth vs Joseph SMITH AB xxx

-      commth vs Obadiah MERRETT gaming
Jury:Thomas KILGORE,William CLARK,John BENTON,Stephen HODGES,Daniel
WITCHER Sr.,Elisha McCOMAS,Joel EASTISS,Patton WALKER,William
WALTON,John EVERITT,Zachariah ESTILL,Noah SCALES   guilty

-      commth vs Jesse BLANKENSHIP AB   costs by Joseph SMITH
-      William McCLUNG vs Samuel NEAL debt -special bail Melchor STROOP
          (LO-says John BROWN (not McClung)vs NEAL)
-      Richd. WHEATLY assee(LO-James RICE) vs Samuel NEAL & Manoah BOSTI(
          special bail Edmd.MORRIS
-      Edmd.McGINNIS vs David CARTMILL case
page 88--------------------
-      (Ammadab SEEKRIGHT)Lessee of(Chester) HOWE & (wife Nancy)
          vs David SPURLOCK   ejectment dism.
-      Robert DOUTHAT vs Henry HAMPTON debt
-      (SEEKRIGHT)Lessee of (Moses)McCORMACK & al(LO-James,Rachael,Sarah,
          Joshua) vs Elizabeth MORGAN & al(Daniel MORGAN) Ejt.
          William COLEMAN made def. & cond. atty David CARTMILL
-      (SEEKRIGHT)Lesee of James T.WATSON vs Wiliam HAMPTON & al
(REATHERFORD, HATTEN,WALKER,WARD,GARRETT) eject.
-      (SEEKRIGHT)Lesee of Elisha McCOMAS vs Ferdinando DREADNOT ejt.
-      (SEEKRIGHT)Lesee of Carter PAGE vs Ferdinando DREADNOT ejt.
          Thomas WARD,John WARD, & Joel ESTIS general of survey
          (affadavits by Hugh BOWEN,John BURTON,Arthur TURLEY judge/plf
no page 89/90
page 91------------   ( ) all added from LO
-      (commth vs Benj.GARRET Jr. & William RUSSELL gaming)
-      (A.SEEKRIGHT for James MADISON heirs vs John COX)

-      (commth & John MORRIS vs Thomas WARD
Jury:Thomas CLAP,Alex.STEPHENSON,William HAMPTON,William MERRITT,Leonard
SHARP,Melchor STROOP,William CLARK,David SPURLOCK,Mark RUSSELL,Ben
MAXEY,John SMITH, James TURLEY & recover costs)

-      (Alex.CATLETT vs John McMAHAN)
-      (same--reverse) wit:Mark RUSSELL,Edmund MORRIS,George WARD)
-      (Jeremiah WARD vs Jacob HITE)
-      (Daniel MORGAN vs William CLARK covt)
-      (Daniel WITCHER Sr. vs Chester HOW)
-      (Richard CRUMP vs Daniel MORGAN & William BARKER debt

```
                wit:John MORRIS Jr.)
  -      deed recorded from Allen PRIOR to Maurice REYNOLDS
                Wednesday 13th Oct 1813  same Judge
  -      commth vs Henry HAMPTON
  -      George DAVIDSON vs Peerson JOHNSON in case
  ------------
  -      Mark RUSSELL vs Henry HAMPTON  Debt
Jury:James MOMAN,Alexander STEPHENSON,DAniel WITCHER Jr.,William
FULLERTON,William McCOMAS,John GRIFFITH,Benjamin DAVIS,Leonard SHARP,
Hugh MILLER,Thoms. CLAP,Daniel WALKER,Sanders WITCHER  find for plf.
debt of 50 pounds + ints. from 1802
page 92------------
  -      William WALTON vs Alexander STEPHENSON AB  special bail Hugh MILLER
  -      James CRESSON(Cripon)  vs John SIMMONS  & Richard CRUMP
                special bail Thos.CLAP
  -      John Osburn LAIDLEY qualified atty
  -      Richard WHEATLEY assee/(James RICE)vs Samuel NEAL & al(M.BOSTICK)
                from Greenup Co.KY deposition of George POAGE & Joseph GARDNER
  -      commth & John MORRIS Jr. vs Thomas WARD  debt
                Sanders WITCHER security
page 93  ------------
  -      Edmund MORRIS clerk    $15
  -      Peter DIRTING jailor   $10
  -      Saml.SHORT sheriff     $10
  -      James WILSON prosecutor  3 days $15
  -      commth vs Obadiah MERRITT(long illegible entry by different clk)
page 94        Superior Court 16th may 1814-Judge James ALLEN
  --------
Grand Jury:Jesse SPURLOCK,William BUFFINGTON,John MORRIS Sr.,William
HAMPTON,Stephen BEAN,Samuel SMILEY,John WELLMAN,John HATFIELD,William
WALTON,Benjamin BROWN,William MORRIS,Peter SCALES,George HOLLANBACK,
Chadw.CHAPMAN,James WILSON,John BURTON,John EVERETT,Samuel CLARK,Isom
GARRETT & James BARRETT & William HOLDERBY
        XXX Daniel MORGAN,Daniel DOUTHAT,William HOLDERBY,Thomas J---XXX
  -      Joseph H.SAMUELS & Joseph LOVELL qualify as atty
  -      commth vs James WILKS AB
  -      commth vs Saml.HUGGANS  AB
page 95------------
  -      commth vs Edward REA   gaming/award (?) to sheriff of Greenbrier
  -      commth vs Chester HOWE    gaming  security William MERRITT
                (Howe commit to Jail)
  -      Robert DOUTHAT  vs Henry HAMPTON & George HOLLANBACK bond
  -      Samuel HENSLEY vs John SIMMONS & Mark RUSSELL bond aga.RUSSELL $325
  -      Thomas EVANS & James LOCKHART assee of John WOODWARD
                vs Henry HAMPTON & c. BOND quashed for information
page 96--------
  -      Saml.HENLEY,Daniel RUFFNER & Joseph RUFFNER
                vs John BARRETT Chancery Court at Staunton order filed
                deposition of Abraham BAKER of Gallia Co.OH taken
  -      commth vs John BURCHAM gaming
  -      commth vs Richd.W.EVANS  murder
  -      commth vs Benjamin GARRETT-security Spencer ELLLIS
  -      commth vs William RUSSELL -security Daniel NEAL
page 97-------
```

28

```
-    commth vs James ADKINS    AB
Jury:Richard TERRELL,William CLARK,Isaac HATFIELD,John GRIFFITH,Leonard
SHARP,William MERRITT,Henry HELPHINSTINE, xx William ADKINSxx,Spencer
ELLIS,Leroy NEWMAN,John EVERETT Jr.,William HATFIELD & John RODGERS
def not guilty
-----------
-    (SEEKRIGHT)Lessee of James WATSON vs William HAMPTON &al ejt.
        (Reatherford,Hatten,Walker,Davis,Ward,Garrett)
-    Joseph SMITH vs Jesse BLANKENSHIP   AB
-    Joshua JONES vs George RODGERS covt-special bail Elisha McCOMAS
-    James CRIPON(Cresson) vs John SIMMONS & Ricahrd CRUMP   debt
-    adm.Sally SIMMONS & Mark RUSSELL   Jury:same as above $.01 damage
        Richard CRUMP the surving obligary(of estate of John SIMMONS)
-    William McCLUNG assee/(John BROWN) vs Samuel NEAL   debt
-    Ammadab SEEKRIGHT lesee of Cartor PAGE vs Thomas WARD & al  ejt
        (John WARD,Joel ESTIS,John BURTON)
-    same            lesse of M.McCORMACK & al vs E.MORGAN,D.MORGAN &
        Wm.COLEMAN)  to Mason Co.
-    Jeremiah WARD vs Jacob HITE &(Nath.SCALES)  debt
page 99-----------
-    George HAIRSTON vs Samuel SHELTON debt
-    Richd.WHEATLY assee/(James RICE)  vs Samuel NEAL &al(M.BOSTICK)
-    Francis TONEY vs Zachariah T.ESTILL   debt
-    (Samuel HENRY,Daniel RUFFNER,Joseph RUFFNER vs John BARRETT)
-    (John CAMPBELL assee/Jacob HEDRICK vs Jeremiah WARD)
-    (Commth vs Micajah BRUMFIELD AB)
-    (Daniel MORGAN vs William CLARK   covenant   spec. bail Henry HAYNIE
Pg 100-----------
-    Greenberry KELLY vs Kenneth BLAKE   case
-    Commth vs Edward REA  AB (grand jury-----
        Tuesday 17th may 1814 same judge as yesterday
(Grand Jury indt.-John WARD       AB
                  Randle ADKINS AB
                  Samuel SHORT   AB
                  John CHAFIN    AB
                  David CHAFIN   AB
                  Edmd.BRAMMER   AB
                  Alex.STEPHENSON AB
                  Danl.WITCHER Jr.AB
                  Elijah STEPHENSON AB
                  Henry BRAMMER  AB
                  John BRAMMER   AB
                  John MEEKS     AB
                  Rollin BIAS    AB
                  Stephen HENSLEY  forgery
-    Jeremiah WARD vs Jacob HITE debt
-    Richard CRUMP vs Daniel MORGAN  debt
-    Nathaniel SCALES vs Thomas WILSON  AB
page 101--------
-    (Philip FAIRPLAY)Lessee of James MADISON heirs (James C.MADISON &
Robert G.SCOTT vs John COX  ejt        Thomas CHAPMAN witness
-----------
-    George DAVIDSON vs Pierson JOHNSON  case
```

Jury:George CHAPMAN,Henry HAYNIE,Elisha McCOMAS,Philip BUMGARDNER,
William CLARK,William MERRITT,Jacob HITE,Jacob STAYLEY,Daniel
MORGAN,James MARKUM,Richard CRUMP & William BARKER for plf $165

- xxGeorge BENTLEYxx,William ALLEN,xxCharles JORDANxx,Alex.PARKERxx
        fined not attending jury

- Daniel MORGAN vs William CLARK covt
Jury:Solomon THORNBURG,John MERRITT,William MARKUM,Reuben SLAUGHTER,
William LOVE,John CAMPBELL,Brice STOKES,George RODGERS,James TURLEY,
William HATFIELD,Leonard SHARP & George DAVIDSON

- (William ALLEN fined for not attending jury)
- Saml.HENRY,Daniel RUFFNER &Joseph RUFFNER
        vs John BARRETT Debt-witness Abraham BAKER of Gallia Co.OH
- William WALTON vs Alexander STEPHENSON AB
- Elisha McCOMAS vs John SMITH trespass
- Joseph WINDON vs William DINGESS debt
Jury:Same as above for plf $166.41
page 103------------ county expenses as before
- (John LONG assee/Edmund McGINNIS vs John BURTON-Wm.LOVE costs)
        Superior Court 17th day Oct 1814-Judge James ALLEN

-Grand Jury:John MORRIS Jr.,Jesse SPURLOCK,Daniel MORGAN,William
BUFFINGTON,Benjamin BROWN,Edmund McGINNIS,John BURTON,William D.MORRIS,
Joseph McGONAGLE,John McCOMAS,Thos.KILGORE,Thomas BUFFINGTON Sr.,John
EVERETT,John EVERRETT Jr.,Noah SCALES,James SMITH,William FULLERTON,
Moses McCORMACK,James McCORMACK,Robert HOLDERBY,Thomas BUFFINGTON,George
HOLLANBACK.--James HOLDERBY & Richard CRUMP fined not attending
page 104--------------
-indt   John HENRY AB
-            John BELLAMY AB
-            Obadiah MERRITT AB
-            Daniel WITCHER Jr. AB
- Joseph WINDON vs William DINGESS debt
- commth vs James WILKS AB
- commth vs Saml.HUGGANS AB
- commth vs Edward REA awarded sheriff of Greenbrier
- commth vs John BURCHAM gaming
- commth vs R.W.EVANS AB
- Commth vs Micajah BRUMFIELD AB
page 105---------
- commth vs John CHAFAN AB
- Commth vs David CHAFAN AB
- commth vs Alexander STEPHENSON AB - awarded to Kanawha Co.
- (commth vs Elijah STEPHENSON AB)
- commth vs Peter DIRTING information

- commth vs John WARD AB
Jury:William SWEARENGIN,William CLARK,Alexander HAZLETT,John FERGUSON,
Littleberry ADKINS,William MILLER,Leonard SWEARINGEN,Obadiah BIAS,
William HAMPTON,John CAMPBELL,James LAFOORE & Benjamin MARTIN
guilty fine 25 cents

- commth vs John MEEKS AB
- commth vs Thos.CHAPMAN rule for contempt/attachment awarded

page 106----------

- commth vs Samuel SHORT same jury (Lewis COLLINS instead/Leonard
        Swearingin) AB def guilty
- commth vs Daniel WITCHER Jr. AB
- commth vs Edmund BRAMMER AB
- commth vs Henry BRAMMER AB same jury (Thos.HILYARD instead of
        Swearginen or Collins)
- commth vs John BRAMMER AB

page 107-------------

- Grand Jury indt.: AB against John HENRY
-                   AB against John BELLAMY
-                   AB against Obadiah MERRITT
-                   AB against Danl.WITCHER Jr. summons each case
- commth vs Randle ADKINS same jury
- commth vs Rolling BIAS AB
- (SEEKRIGHT)Lessee of James T.WATSON vs William HAMPTON & al(Robert
REATHERFORD,Asa HATTON,William WALKER,Paul DAVIS,Thomas WARD,Joseph
GARRETT ejt dismissed

- (SEEKRIGHT)Lessee/Saml.M.HOPKINS &(James WATSON)
        vs Ferdinando DREANOT
Jury:Thomas WARD,William HAMPTON,William WALKER,Asa HATTON,Edward
PAULEY,Benjamin GARRETT Sr.,Saml.FERGUSON,Paul DAVIS,Robert REATHERFORD,
Joseph GARRETT,William CLARK,Alexander HAZLETT

Pg 108------------

- Daniel RUFFNER & al(Joseph RUFFNER & Samuel HENRY)
        vs John BARRETT debt
- Joseph SMITH vs Jesse BLAKENSHIP AB-------
        Tuesday 18th Oct 1814 same judge
- George HAIRSTON vs Saml.SHELTON debt David SPURLOCK special bail
- commth vs Thomas CHAPMAN rule for contempt/set aside
- Thomas EVANS & James LOCKHEART
        vs Reuben SLAUGHTER & Goodrich SLAUGHTER AB

page 109-----------

- Philip FAIRPLAY lesse of MADISON heirs vs John COX ejt
Jury:Daniel SPURLOCK,Jeremiah WELLMAN,John FERGUSON,James BARRETT,
Cadwalldader CHAPMAN,Daniel DOUTHAT,George RODGERS,John McCOMAS,John
MORRIS Jr.,Joseph McGONAGLE,Kenneth BLAKE,William McCOMAS

- Joshua JONES vs George RODGERS covt
Jury:Daniel SPURLOCK,John FERGUSON,Cadwallader CHAPMAN,Daniel DOUTHAT,
John MORRIS Jr.,Joseph McGONAGLE,Kenneth BLAKE,William McCOMAS,William
CLARK,James SNODGRASS,William GREENWOOD,Jeremiah WELLMAN
for the plf $57.92 damages with interest from 1810

- (SEEKRIGHT)lessee of Elisha McCOMAS vs John SMITH ejt
- (SEEKRIGHT)lessee of Carter PAGE vs Thomas WARD & al (John
WARD,Joel ESTIS,Arthur TURLEY,John BURTON)

page 110--------------

- Elisha McCOMAS vs John SMITH trespass
- Greenberry KELLY vs Kenneth BLAKE-Greenup Co.KY to take deposition
        of James RICE & Alex.CATLETT

31

```
-       William WALTON vs Alexander STEPHENSON   AB
Jury:same jury (John CAMPBELL instead of Snodgrass)
-       John LONG (assee of Edmd.McGINNIS) vs John BURTON debt
-       John CAMPBELL (assee of Jacob HENDRICK) vs Jeremiah WARD   debt
page 111---------------
-       George HAIRSTON vs Saml.SHELTON    AB
Jury:Edmund McGINNIS,William SWEARINGEN,James WILSON,John WELLMAN,
Thomas CHAPMAN,Jacob MARKUM,Thomas HATFIELD,John EVERETT Jr.,John
BURTON, Thomas KILGORE,John EVERETT Sr.,James CONNER find for plf
-------------
-       Richard WHEATLEY assee(of James RECE) vs Saml.NEAL debt
Jury:Edmund McGINNIS,William SWEARINGEN,James WILSON,John WELLMAN, Jacob
MARKUM,Thomas HATFIELD,John BURTON, Thomas KILGORE,John EVERETT
Sr.,James CONNER  Andrew HUGGARD,Stephen HENSLEY,John MORRIS Jr.
------------------
        George WARD (assee of Henry HAYNIE) vs John RODGERS
            William CLARK special bail
-       Leonard SWEARINGEN   vs   Daniel WALKER   covt
page 112-----------
-       lessee of James MADISON heirs vs John COX  ejt
            deposition of Thomas HUFF of KY
-       Francis TONEY    vs Zachariah ESTILL  AB
-       James WILSON vs James MARKUM   AB
JURY:Edmund McGINNIS,Thos.HATFIELD,Andrew HUGGAND,John CAMPBELL,James
CONNER,John BURTON,Thomas KILGORE,John EVERETT Sr.,John MORRIS Jr.,
Stephen HENSLEY,William GREENWOOD,&Kenneth BLAKE---
Jeremiah WELLMAN & Samuel SMILEY rule for contempt
-----------------------
-       Charles LOVE vs Mark RUSSELL   DEBT
-       commth vs Wm.ALLEN  fined for missing jury duty
page 113---------
-       Samuel WARD vs Jacob HITE & Nathl.SCALES  debt
            special bail Edmund McGINNIS------
            WEDNESDAY 19TH OCT 1814    same judge
-       Ammadab SEEKRIGHT lessee of HOPKINS(& James T.WATSON) vs Wm.HAMPTON
(Thomas WARD,William WALKER,Asa HATTON,Edward PAULEY,Benjamin GARRETT
Sr.,Samuel FERGUSON Sr.,Paul DAVIS,Robert REATHERFORD,Joseph GARRETT,
William CLARK, A.HAZELETT.)ejt venue changed to Mason Co.  Edmund MORRIS
security
----------------
-       John EVERETT Sr. vs Charles RAMSEY  case
Jury:William McCOMAS,John WELLMAN,George RODGERS,David McCOMAS,William
McCOMAS Jr.,John McCOMAS,James TURLEY,Benjamin RICH,Stephen HENSLEY,
Daniel SPURLOCK,Andrew CHAPMAN,David FRENCH  new trial awarded
----------------
-       C.R.MANEGAR vs William MERRITT  debt
page 114-------------
-       George WARD assee (OF Henry HAYNIE) vs McCOWN & RODGERS   debt
-       Jeremiah WARD vs Jacob HITE  & N.SCALES debt
------------
-       William DINGESS vs Richard TERRELL   covt
Jury:John IRVIN,John SMITH,John EVERETT Jr.,Edmund McGINNIS,John EVERETT
Sr.,John CAMPBELL,William GREENWOOD,Elijah SIMMONS,John HARRY(Henry),
James THOMPSON,Thomas CHILDERS & Rufus LEONARD  plf damages
```

```
------------
-     Squire THOMPSON assee(of Henry FARLEY)  vs Thomas McCOMAS  covt
Jury : same (Samuel SHORT instead of John Smith)
pg 115-------------
      County allowances same as before
-     Samuel SMILEY & Jeremiah WELLMAN fine set aside
          Superior Court 15th day of May 1815 Judge James ALLEN
-     Dower commission examined Agatha S.PAYTON to deed of bargain from
          John H.PAYTON recorded
--------------
-Grand Jury:Edmund McGINNIS,Benjamin BROWN,William BUFFINGTON,Thomas
BUFFINGTON JR.,John WELLMAN,Jesse TONEY,James MAYO,Noah SCALES,John
HANNAN,Daniel DAVIS,James SMITH,Daniel FRANCE,Thomas KILGORE,Elisha
McCOMAS,John EVERETT Sr.,John SMITH,Ezekiel SMITH,Henry HATCHER,William
DAVIS,William HAMPTON & Stephen BEAN--Peter SCALES & Thomas MORRIS fined
page 116--------
-     commth vs Edward REA  gaming
-     commth vs John BURCHAM gaming
-     C.R.MENEGAR vs William MERRITT  bond
------------------
-     commth vs Peter DIRTING information as jailor
Jury:Peter LOVE,Adam SMITH,Stephen MARKUM,Leonard SWEARENGIN,Robert
BOULT(Samuel SMILEY)John BURTON,Danl.WITCHER Jr.,Edward BRAMMER,James
TURLEY,Stephen WILSON,George CHAPMAN,James WILSON   not guilty
William BRUMLEY fined for not attending
--------------
-     commth vs Richard W.EVANS indt for murder
NEW SUMMONS AWARDED IN EACH OF THE FOLLOWING:
Page 117------------
      commth vs Micajah BRUMFIELD   AB  (summons Giles Co.)
          "     Edward REA
          "     John CHAFAN
          "     David CHAFAN
          "     Alex.STEPHENSON
          "     John MEEKS
          "     John HENRY
EACH   OF FOLLOWING FOUND NOT GUILTY
-     commth vs John BELLAMY
-             Obadiah MERRITT
-             Daniel WITCHER Jr.
-             Elijah STEPHENSON
PAGE 118------------------
-     commth vs Edmund BRAMMER
Jury:William FULLERTON,Daniel WITCHER Sr.,Israel HEATH,George RODGERS,
William BRUMFIELD,David McCOMAS Jr.Thomas CHILDERS John GILKERSON,Philip
BUMGARDNER,William TONEY,Charles RAMSEY & James RAY not guilty
--------------
-     lessee of Carter PAGE(SEEKRIGHT)
          vs WARD & al ejectment -Arthur TURLLEY def
-     commth vs James HOLDERBY & Richard CRUMP not  attend Grand Jury
-     NIELL & HURLEY  vs Sally SIMMONS  debt
GRAND JURY indt: Harris PRIOR gaming
-             James HANGER spiritious liquors
-             John DINGESS same
```

```
-        Wm.DINGESS      same
-        Edward PAULEY   AB
-        William BURNES  AB
-        Hastin FRAZER   AB
-        John SHELTON    AB
-        Edward FRANKLIN AB
-        Charles JORDAN  AB  summons for each  COURT AJOURNED
PAGE 120------------      Tuesday 16th May 1816  same judge
-    Sally WILBURN vs Danl.WALKER  case
---------------
-        commth vs Daniel WITCHER Jr.  indt
```
Jury:Fredrick HAYNER,William TONEY,James TURLLEY,Leonard SWEARENGIN,
Absalom HOLDERBY,Ezekiel SMITH,Charles RAMSEY,James SMITH ,William
BRUMFIELD,John EVERETT Sr.,Stephen MARKUM,William WALTON guilty $30

-    William HAMPTON vs Stephen BEAN case

-    Commth vs Daniel WITCHER Jr. indt AB
Jury:William CLARK,William MERRITT,Stephen STALEY,George CHAPMAN,David
McCOMAS Jr.,John MERRETT,John CANTRIL,Elijah SEAMONS,Littleberry ADKINS,
Samuel SHORT,Robert (BAUL) & Hezekiah ADKINS guilty
30 days imprisonment $500 and security

-    commth vs John BRAMMER indt AB
Jury:Saml.BARRETT,James BIAS,Obadiah MERRETT,John GILKERSON,John
HUDDLESTON,James WHITE,Jesse TONEY,Ezekiel SMITH,John EVERETT Sr.,
William TONEY,William BRUMFIELD & Leonard SWEARENGIN guilty $1

-    commth vs Rollin BIAS indt AB
Jury:John BELLAMY,Stephen WILSON,Elisha McCOMAS,James SMITH,James
TURLEY,Noah SCALES,James CONNER,Andrew BARRETT,Thomas CHILDERS,Henry
HATCHER, & Daniel WITCHER Sr.& Edmund McGINNIS not guilty
PAGE 122--------------
-    Rule vs Hugh BOWEN being absent from court

-    commth vs John BELLAMY indt AB
Jury:Stephen WILSON,Elisha McCOMAS,James SMITH,James TURLEY,Noah SCALES,
James CONNER,Andrew BARRETT,Thos.CHILDERS,Henry HATCHER,Daniel WITCHER
Sr.,James THOMPSON,John HANNAN not guilty

-    lessee of MADISON heirs(FAIRPLAY) vs John COX ejectment
Jury:William CLARK,William MERRITT,Stephen STALEY,George CHAPMAN,David
McCOMAS Jr.,John BARRETT,John CANTRIL,Elijah SEAMONDS,Littleberry
ADKINS, Hezekiah ADKINS,John EVERITT Sr.,William TONEY

-    Mary HAYNER vs Thomas CONLEY case
page 123------------------
-    William BRUMLEY fine set aside
          Wednesday 17th day May 1815 same Judge------------------
-    Daniel RUFFNER & al vs John BARRETT debt
Jury,William BUFFINGTON,Samuel SMILEY,Charles RAMSEY,Elijah SEAMONDS,
William TONEY,Jesse TONEY,Ezekiel SMITH,John EVERRITT Sr.,Samuel
HUDDLESTON,John HANNAN,Kenneth BLAKE,George CHAPMAN

- Leonard SWEARINGEN vs DAniel WALKER covt

- lessee of Elisha McCOMAS vs John SMITH ~ejt
    Thomas WARD & Noah SCALES defts for Smith
Jury:Edmund McGINNIS,William CLARK,James WILSON,Obadiah MERRITT,John
HENRY,Joseph McGONAGLE,Thomas IRVIN,Jesse SPURLOCK,Andrew BARRETT,John
BARRETT,Adam BLACK,James McGINNIS con't
page 124------------
- (SEEKRIGHT)lessee of Carter PAGE vs Thomas WARD & al ejt
- Greenberry KELLY vs Kenneth BLAKE appt
- lessee of Elisha McCOMAS vs John SMITH trespass
- John EVERITT SR. vs Charles RAMSEY trespass
Jury: same(Joel ESTIS instead of James Wilson)

- George WARD assee of Henry HAYNIE vs John RODGERS covt
Jury:Hezekiah ADKINS Jr.,Thos.CHILDERS,Nathaniel EVERETT,(Wm.FULLERTON)
William BUFFINGTON,Samuel SMILEY,Charles RAMSEY,William TONEY,John
EVERITT Sr.,Kenneth BLAKE,James McGINNIS,James WILSON,Allen RECE
FOR PLF $112.50 with inst from 1811

- Chester HOWE vs Littleberry ADKINS case
Jury:same (Nathan EVERITT instead of Hez.Adkins) non suit
- Stephen WILSON vs Daniel WITCHER AB
- Charles STUART vs Archd.BLANKENSHIP AB
page 126-----------
- Kenneth BLAKE vs Stephen KELLY AB
- Danl.WITCHER Sr. vs DAniel WITCHER Jr. case--con't
- Nathl.CUSHING vs Daniel NEAL debt
- George COUNTS vs William WALKER(Charles WALKER,George DAVIDSON,John
McMAHAN,Daniel MORGAN) debt

    Thursday 17th May 1815 same judge
    Mark RUSSELL sheriff $10.00
    Edmd.MORRIS clk   15.00
    Peter DIRTING jailor 10.00
    James WILSON pros.   4 days
page 127-------------
- rule against Hugh BOWEN for not appearing at Court
- John EVERETT vs Charles RAMSEY trespass
- Lessee of Elisha McCOMAS vs Thomas WARD & Noah SCALES ejt
     referred to Henry WHITE & Joseph LOVEL

    SUPERIOR COURT 16th day Oct 1815 Judge James ALLEN
     John (Irvin) appointed protem clerk
-Grand Jury:Edmund McGINNIS,John MORRIS Jr.,Thomas KILGORE,Sampson
SANDERS,Cadwallader CHAPMAN,William GREENWOOD,Thomas McCOLUTER, Lawrence
BRYANT,Andrew GUIN,Thomas MORRIS,Pyrres McGINNIS,John CARTER,Jesse
SPURLOCK,Daniel MORGAN,Manoah BOSTICK,Richard BROWN,REuben ADKINS,Daniel
DAVIS,Jacob HITE,William HITE,Joseph HILYARD,George HOLLENBACK,Daniel
DOUTHAT & James McGINNIS.
page 128----------
- Littleberry ADKINS vs Chester HOWE bond
- Jeremiah WARD vs Jacob HITE & Nathl.SCALES,(Peter SCALES)
    Bond/illegally taken

-    commth vs James BARRETT
-    Kenneth BLAKE vs Stephen KELLY bond
-   Squire THOMPSON vs Thomas McCOMAS,David McCOMAS,&William ADKINS bond

page 129-----------
-    commth vs Edward REA gaming   (Mason Co.)
-    commth vs John BURCHAM   gaming
-    commth vs Richd.W.EVANS   murder
-    commth vs Micajah BRUMFIELD   AB (Giles Co.

page 130 & 131

-    commth vs John CHAFIN AB : David CHAFIN AB :Alex.STEPHENSON AB
-John MEEKS   AB : Jno.HENRY AB : James HOLDERBY (Not att.G.Jury) :
-Richard CRUMP (not att.G.Jury): James HANGER liquor :Edward PAULY AB
-William DINGESS liquor : John DINGESS liquor : William BURRIS AB(died)
-Edward FRANKLIN AB : John SHELTON AB : Harris PRIOR gaming : Charles
-JORDAN AB : Hasten FRASIER AB

page 132-------------
-    Daniel WITCHER Jr. adm of L.WITCHER vs Jeremiah WARD case
-    John BURTON vs John STONE debt Thomas WARD for deft
-Grand Jury presents: Alexander SOUTHERLAND malfeazance in office
                  William BRUMFIELD AB

-    commth vs Elijah STEPHENSON AB
Jury:Henry HATCHER, Andrew BARRETT, William BRUMFIELD, William MILLER,
Elisha McCOMAS, George CHAPMAN, John FULLERTON, James HOLDERBY, John SMITH,
John DINGESS, Ransom DIAL not guilty

pg 133--------
-    Saml.HINCH vs   John WALLACE case

-    commth vs Obadiah MERRITT AB
Jury:Solomon HENSLEY, William HATFIELD, John SAMPLE, Charles RAMSEY, Thomas
HATFIELD, Adam SMITH, John FULLERTON, John HATFIELD, Henry HATCHER, Joseph
HILYARD, Moses McCOMAS & William BRUMFIELD guilty $.01

-    Alex,SOUTHERLAND & William BRUMFIELD order by Court to appear
-    Benja.BROWN(Thomas EVANS,James LOCKHEART) vs Reuben SLAUGHTER
      (& Goodbridge SLAUGHTER) counter security
-    commth vs Daniel WITCHER Jr. AB same jury guilty $.01

page 134--------------- Thursday 17th day Oct 1816
-    Lessee of Elisha McCOMAS vs Thomas WARD & Noah SCALES ejt
     refered to Joseph SAMUELS,Henry WHITE, John LAIDLEY

-    James BARRETT brought into court by jailor-stands indt for passing
        counterfeit money
Jury:Jesse McCOMAS, William McCOMAS, Isaac McCOMAS, David McCOMAS, Ransom
DIAL, David PATTEN, Ezekiel SMITH, John DINGESS, John WISHON, Reuben
SLAUGHTER,& William ADKINS not guilty

page 135-------
-    Charles STUART VS Archibald BLANKENSHIP note for AB
Jury:William HATFIELD, Bird BRUMFIELD, Andrew BARRETT, John SMITH, John
FERGUSON, Elisha McCOMAS, John BURNS, Rolen BIAS, John NEWMAN, Jacob
STALEY, Samuel HUDDLESTON, Stephen HENSLEY not guilty

-    Henry SPIERS vs Israel HEATH

-xx   Stephen WILSON vs Danl.WITCHER Jr.
-      Ammadab SEEKRIGHT on demise of Rich.REYNOLDS & Saml.HINCH
          vs Ferdinando DREADNOT- Adam HATFIELD for def
page 136---------
-      Thomas EVANS Jr.(& James LOCKHEART assee of John WOODARD vs Reuben
SLAUGHTER (& Goodbridge SLAUGHTER) motion for execution
                Wednesday 18th Oct 1815---------
-      Danl.RUFFNER vs John BARRETT debt
Jury:Edmund McGINNIS,Jesse RAY,Joseph McGONAGLE,Nathan CARDWELL,James
RAY,John FERGUSON,Stephen HENSLEY,John SMITH,David McCOMAS,William
McCOMAS,James THOMPSON,Benjamin JOHNSTON

-      (SEEKRIGHT)Lessee of Elisha McCOMAS vs John SMITH ejt
page 137----------
-      Lessee of Carter PAGE vs(xxCarter Page)Thomas WARD & Co.
Jury:Ezekiel SMITH,John BARRETT,Charles RAMSEY,Elisha McCOMAS,Thomas
HATFIELD,Saml.HUDDLESTON,William HATFIELD,Reuben SLAUGHTER,William
FULLERTON,John MORRIS,Andrew BARRETT,John EVERETT find for def
----
-          Thursday 19th OCT 1815   Same judge---
-      Greenberry KELLY vs Kenneth BLAKE case
Jury:John EVERETT Jr.,Ezekiel SMITH,Elijah SEAMONDS,William FULLERTON,
Roland BIAS,John EVERETT Sr.,George SPIERS,Henry PAYTON,John SMITH,
William HATFIELD,John BARRETT,(HAMPTON)Elisha McCOMAS for plf $100
PAGE 138

-      Elisha McCOMAS vs John SMITH trespass
-      John EVERITT Sr. vs Charles RAMSEY trespass
-      Daniel WITCHER Sr. vs Daniel WITCHER Jr. case
def. saith that if such words were uttered they were by intoxication
----
-      NIELL & HURLEY vs Sally SIMMONS
same jury except Hugh (?)Plyton) for McComas)
evidence by John HENRY & Jn.MATHERS dep.of BAKER
page 139--------
-XX   Danl.WITCHER adm.(& assee of Sanders WITCHER) vs Jeremiah WARD
xxJury:John EVERETT Sr.,Sam.HUDDLESTON + same as above xx

-      Danl.WITCHER adm vs Jerh.WARD
Jury:John EVERETT Sr.,Sam;.HUDDLESTON,Ezekiel SMITH,Elijah SEAMONDS,
William FULLERTON,Roland BIAS,John EVERETT Jr.,George SPIERS,Henry
PEYTON,John SMITH,William HATFIELD,John BARRETT for plf $65

-      James SMITH & (Ginny SMITH) vs James FULLERTON case
Jury:Edmd.McGINNIS,James CONNER,Jesse RAY,James McGINNIS,Joel ESTIS,
Benjamin JOHNSON,Daniel DAVIS,Nathan EVERITT,Charles RAMSEY,Samuel
BARRETT,Jonathan PEYTON,Samuel HINCH for plf $150
page 140--------------
-      Henry SPEARS vs Israel HEATH
Jury:Danl.DOUTHAT,Andrew BARRETT,Nathan CARDWELL,Philip BAUMGARDNER,
John WARD,James McGONANGLE,Chester HOW,Wm.MERRITT,Chas.WILSON, Patrick
MORRISON,Thomas HATFIELD,James THOMPSON -Barrett dismissed Jury released
----
-      Geo.RODGERS vs Jerh.WARD

```
-      Israel HEATH vs Henry SPEARS
-      Saml.HINCH vs John WALLACE
PAGE 141----------
-      Stephen WILSON vs Danl.WITCHER Jr.
-      Samuel SMILEY vs Henry FARLER & Stephen HENSLEY debt
-      John BURTON vs John STONE debt
-      Wm.McCLUNG assee(John BROWN) vs Melchor STROOP
-      Jas.BOLT(assee of Adam SMITH) vs John BURTON
-      (SEEKRIGHT demise of Thos.BUFFINGTON & Wm.BUFFINGTON vs Ferdinando
DREADNAUGHT on affadvits of William HATCHER,Robert ADAMS in possession)
-      Mark RUSSELL sheriff
       Geo.MERRITT jailor
       John SAMUELS clerk pro tem (2 oct 1815)
       James WILSON pro.atty
-      Danl.WITCHER adm.(& assee of Sanders WITCHER) vs Jeremiah WARD
          wit:Edmd.McGINNIS & Pleasant HAZLEWOOD
             (PAGE 125 IS END OF LO 1812-1815 page 126 begins 1816)
page 142---------------
       Friday   20th Oct 1815(see forward a few pages
(FORMAT CHANGES as each entry is underlined in a box on double page)
page 143
```

Persons Named	delivered	amount	sheriff return	ses
-William PERRY vs John FANNIN	R.CRUMP	debt ints from 1809-Costs $200		May
-Robert TABOUR vs Henry FARLEY	sheriff	fifa costs 122 conts & $5	two late came --hand John WARD DS Thos.WARD SCC	
-Charles BOOTH vs Nancy DROWN	sheriff	fifa 122 conts & $5	satisfied J.WARD DS T.WARD SCC	
-John SMITH vs Benjamin DAVIS	sheriff	fifa costs $2.28 conts	Exon returned to office without anything being said	July

```
page 144-45
```

- James MOMAN & wife shf vs William TONEY Sr.		damage $1 $44.96 & $2.50	satisfied J.WARD & T.WARD	dec
- commth vs Thos.WARD	coroner	costs $6.63 & $2.94	exon sat.prior CCC Edmd.MORRIS	dec
- commth vs John SIMMONS	shf	costs $5.63 & $2.94	prosecutor & clk Thomas WARD	dec
- commth vs Wm.HOLDERBY Jr.	shf	same	satisfied Ward &Ward	

- .commth vs Wm.MERRIT Jr.	shf	same	same	dec
- commth vs Richd.CRUMP	shf	same	same	
- commth vs James HOGAN	shf	$2.57 & 15	property taken	
- Saml.STEPHENSON vs John FULLERTON		$3.91	same	
- James MILLER vs Wm.& Robt.TABOUR for benefit Alex CATLETT		$90.30 $.73 & 15	sat. by sale of property Thos.WARD	
- commth vs James HOGAN	shf	$2.97 & 15	satisfied Ward & Ward	
- Edward BARRETT vs Isaac HATFIELD		$10 damage 10% from 1810	property taken but no bidders Ward & Ward	

page 146------- (CHANGE AGAIN)
- Thomas WARD vs John HANNAN case / for plf Danl.WITCHER Sr., David McCOMAS, Elisha McCOMAS, Jesse SPURLOCK, Sanders WITCHER, John SHELTON, Peter DIRTING, and Thomas WARD each 3 day attendance
----
- commth vs John MORRIS Jr. information for def./Richard BROWN, Thomas CLAP

- commth vs Richard CRUMP /David McCOMAS 2 days witness for plf
----
- commth vs Thos.KILGORE /Charles ALSBURY 2 days plf William FULLERTON 2 days for plf
----
- commth vs John SIMMONS /Henry BROWN 2 days plf

- J.MOOMAN vs Wm.TONEY /Mathis McCOWN 2 days & 21 miles Edmund BRYSON & Rebeckah BRYSON for plf 2 days 155 miles & 12 1/2 cents each Tenniages(?)

- commth vs J.SIMMONS /Mark RUSSELL 2 day for plf

- commth vs Obadiah BIAS /James WILSON 1 DAY

PAGE 148 Commonwealth causes to Oct term 1809

- commth vs William JORDAN (most discharged for costs)
- vs J.BIARS
- vs T.WARD
- T.KILGORE
- S.SHORT
- W.MERRITT
- W.HOLDERBY
- J.SIMMONS

```
-              R.CRUMP
-              W.GREENWOOD
-              C.HOW
-              N.DROWN
-              J.RODGERS
-              J.FULLERTON
-              J.JONES
-              P.BARHEART
```

PAGE 149   Issue to Oct term 1809

```
-    Jas.MOMAN (2 days) vs W.TONEY judgement
-    EVANS & al vs HAMPTON & al
-    G.HOLLANDBACK vs T.WARD case
-    M.BOSTICK vs W.MERRIT
-    Thos.WARD vs J.HANNAN case
```
----
page 150   commonwealth causes May term 1810

```
-    commth vs Wm.JORDEN & al    jury verdict for def
-              J.BIARS & al       jury verdict & judg.for commth
-              T.KILGORE          jury for def
-              S.SHORT            jury for commth
-              W.GREENWOOD        jury for def
-              C.HOW              information ordered
-              N.DROWN            same
-              J.RODGERS          discharged
-              J.FULLERTON        same
-              J.JONES            same
-              P.BARNHEART        same
-              J.HOGAN            indt quashed
-              T.CHAPMAN          discharged
-              J.FURGUSON         same
-    S.HOLLAND(free mulatto)      same
-              J.MORRIS Jr.       information ordered
```
----
page 151   commth causes 1st day OCT TERM 181-(1810)

```
-         commth vs Samuel SHORT
-                   Chester HOW
-                   Nancy DROWN
-                   John MORRIS JR.
-                   Obadiah MERRETT
-2ND DAY Manoah BOSTICK      vs William MERRETT
-    Thomas EVANS & al vs Henry HAMPTON
-    Thomas WARD         vs John HANNAN
-    Henry HAMPTON Jr. vs James HOGAN
```

PAGE 152 Rule Ind. & Disour. to Order   Oct 181-(1810)
```
-    Daniel RUFFNER vs John BARRETT  indt for debt
-    Manoah BOSTICK vs William MERRIT dismissed
-    Elizabeth SHELTON vs Sampson SANDERS dismissed
-    Sampson SANDERS vs Elizabeth SHELTON dismissed
-    Alex.PORTER      vs Jeremiah WARD  dismissed
```

```
-     Jeremiah WARD   vs David DOUTHAT  discontinued
-.    David DOUTHAT   vs Jeremiah WARD  dismissed
```

```
page 153/154   Trial Docket Commth  causes  May Term 1811
        plf & def                plf witness
- commth vs Samuel SHORT
-            John MORRIS Jr.
-            Obadiah MERRITT       Charles BOOTH & William FULLERTON def
-            Sanders WITCHER       Jacob HITE
-            Daniel NEAL           Jacob HITE
-      XX    Thos.CLAP
-            Daniel WITCHER Jr.    Jesse SPURLOCK & Sampson SANDERS
-            John BYERS Jr.        Sampson SANDERS
-            Charles STUART        Wm.BUFFINGTON & Charles LOVE
-            Hugh MILLER           Wm.DINGESS & Elisha McCOMAS
-            George RODGERS        Wm.DINGESS & Elisha McCOMAS
-            Moses MOTT            Jacob HITE
-            Robert HOLDERBY       Daniel DOUTHAT
-            Daniel NEAL           Jesse SPURLOCK & Sampson SANDERS
-            Thomas CLAP
-            James WILKS           William BUFFINGTON
-            James WILKS           Daniel DOUTHAT
-            Samuel HUGGANS        Sampson SANDERS
-            James BYERS           Jacob HITE
-            John HOLLANDBACK      Martin HOLLANDBACK
-            Samuel FERGUSON       Wm.SPURLOCK & John FERGUSON
-            Jonathan BUFFINGTON   Henry FRANCE & James MOMAN
-            Patsy WHITECOTTON     Henry FRANCE & James MOMAN
```

```
PAGE 155    Issues to May term 1811
      plf & def          plf witness              def witness
- Thomas EVANS &al
  vs Henry HAMPTON & al
```

```
- Thomas WARD            D.McCOMAS, E.McCOMAS,    R.BROWN, Thomas CLAP,
  vs John HANNAN           N.SCALES, J.BARRETT,     Jas.MOMAN, W.DUNBARE,
                         G.WARD, P.DIRTING,       J.LEE, John MORRIS Sr.,
                         Jesse SPURLOCK, Natl.    Spencer ALHERSON, R.TULL,
                         SCALES, D.WITCHER Jr.,   P.DIRTING, Stephen RIGGS
                         J.TURLEY, J.RUSSELL,     Jas.SHELTON, Henry HAYNIE
                         J.GRIFFITH, D.NEAL,
                         S.WITCHER, T.CLAP,
                         W.SPURLOCK, Joel ESTIS   jury verdict for plf
```

```
-   Daniel RUFFNER  vs John BARRETT   cond
```

```
              APPEALS May TERM 1811
-   Mark RUSSELL vs Thomas WARD
-   John SIMMONS vs William BUFFINGTON  to establish ferry
-   Henry HAMPTON vs James HOGAN
-   George DAVIDSON vs Pierson JOHNSON
-   Thomas BUFFINGTON vs William HOLDERBY Sr.
```

```
        SUITS FOR SECOND DAY OF THE TERM
```

41

```
            Suits standing on writs of Enquiry at May term 1811
  -         Richard BROWN vs Thomas WARD
  -         George DAVIDSON vs Brice STOKES
  ---------------------------------------------------------------------
            RULE DISMISSED TO MAY TERM 1811
  -         Daniel WITCHER Sr. vs Thomas WARD
  -         Alex.CATLETT Sr. vs James HOGAN
  ---------------------------------------------------------------------
Page 156/7/8  CABELL COUNTY SUPERIOR COURT 1st day causes Oct term 1811
  ---------------------------------------------------------------------

        plf & def                  plf witness
 -commth vs John MORRIS Jr.
  -      vs Obadiah MERRITT
  -      vs Sanders WITCHER        Charles BOOTH & William FULLERTON
         vs Daniel NEAL            Jacob HITE
  -      vs Daniel WITCHER Jr.     Jesse SPURLOCK, Sampson SANDERS
  -      vs John BYERS Jr.         Sampson SANDERS
  -      vs Charles STUART         Wm.BUFFINGTON ,Charles (?)ink
  -      vs Hugh MILLER            William DINGESS,Elisha McCOMAS
  -      vs George RODGERS         William DINGESS,Elisha McCOMAS
  -      vs Moses MOTT             Jacob HITE
  -      vs Daniel NEAL            Jesse SPURLOCK,Sampson SANDERS
  -      vs James WILKS            Daniel DOUTHAT
  -      vs Samuel HUGGANS         Sampson SANDERS
  -      vs James BYERS            Jacob HITE
  -      vs John HOLLANDBACK       Martin HOLLANDBACK
  -      vs Samuel FURGUSON        Wm.SPURLOCK,John FERGUSON
  -      vs Jonathan BUFFINGTON    Henry FRANCE,& James MOMAN
  -      vs Patsy WHITECOTTON      Henry FRANCE ,James MOMAN
  -      vs James HOLDERBY
  -      vs George WARD            Horatio CATLETT,Richard CRUMP,
                                   G.DAVIDSON,W.BRUMFIELD
  -      Peter COFFEE              James POTEET ,W.MORRIS
  -      James HEPHINSON(Stephenson) Jacob FUDGE & John MORRIS Jr
  -      James POTEET              Peter COFFLE & William MORRIS-
  ---------------------------------------------------------------------
complete duplication 148-179
    The following pages are a reinteration of the previous information.
    The only difference is the grid form on which they are recorded.
    Many cases are continued several times before settlement.
    To save duplication and space, cases are only repeated if there is
    different information each time----------------
  ---------------------------------------------------------------------
page 179    commth cases MAY TERM 1816 first day causes
  -              commth vs Edward REA        gaming
  -                      John BURCHAM        gaming
  -                      Richard W.EVANS     murder
  -                      Micajah BRUMFIELD   AB
  -                      David CHAFEN        AB
  -                      Alexander STEPHENSON AB
  -                      John MEEKS          AB
  -                      John HENRY          AB
  -                      Richard CRUMP       NO Grand Jury
  -                      James HAGER         liquor
```

```
-pg180                          Edward PAULEY          "
-                               William DINGESS        "
-                               John DINGESS           "
-                               Edward FRANKLIN       AB
-                               John SHELTON          AB
-                               Harris PRIOR        gaming
-                               Charles JORDAN        AB
-                               Hasten FRAZIER        AB
-                               William BRUMFIELD     AB
-                               Alexander SOUTHERLAND  malfieance
        2nd day causes & writs of inquiry
-               Stephen WILSON  vs Daniel WITCHER Jr.
-       lesse of Wm.BUFFINGTON & Thos.BUFFINGTON vs Robt.ADAMS  ejt
-               John IRWIN      vs Joseph McGONIGLE  Debt
-               Roland BIAS     vs Pattsey JOHNSON
-               Daniel WITCHER Jr. vs Stephen WILSON
-               GALLAGHER & WARD   vs Moses & David McCOMAS
-               John TIERNAN assee vs Thomas WARD,John BURTON,John STONE
        Judgments & dismmissions
-               James GALLAHER  vs Thomas WARD
-               Edmund MORRIS asseee vs William HITE
-               John EVERETT SR.vs Charles RAMSEY
-               Henry SPIERS    vs Isreal HEATH
-               John CHADWICK   vs William HAMPTON
-               Isreal HEATH    vs Henry SPIERS
-               Philip BALLARD  vs Samuel MUNSEY
-               John JANNEY     vs Robt.ADAMS
-               Joshua JOHNSON vs Stephen KELLY
-               Daniel WITCHER Sr. vs James HOLDERBY
PAGE 181  1st day causes OCT term 1816
        commth vs same (add)
-                       Edward RECE    gaming
-                       John BURCHAM   gaming
-                       Rich.W.EVANS   murder
-                       Thomas MORRIS trespass & liquor
-                       James ALDRIDGE liquor
-                       Benjamin SMITH liquor
-page 182    "     Stephen KELLY
-                       William HAMPTON
        CIVIL SUITS
-       Ammadab SEEKRIGHT demise of Richard REYNOLDS & Samuel HINCH
                vs Adam HATFIELD,Thomas HATFIELD ,William HATFIELD,
                David OUSELEY ,John HATFIELD  ejt
        writs of enquiry
-       George RODGERS vs Jeremiah WARD
-       James WILSON    vs Edmund MORRIS
-       Christen Frederick CORDEMAN vs George CHAPMAN
-       Lewis(by his mother Milly)McGINNIS
                vs William FULLERTON & Jane RODGERS
        Judgements & dismissions
-       William PRATT & John ARTHUR assee of David J.WOOD
                vs William WALKER,James WILSON,Robert WILSON
-       Robert GARRETT vs Benja.WHITE
-       Hughs CAPERTON Sr.&Henry ALEXANDER assee of John COOK Sr.
```

```
              (who was assee of John COOK Jr.) vs William DINGESS
    -     George WARD vs Richard CRUMP
    -     Benjamin BROOK vs William WALKER &James STUART
    -     James GALLAHER assee of Edward MILLER
              vs William & Charles WALKER
    -     George WARD assee of John McMAHAN
              vs William CLARK & George HOLLENBACK
    -     Jeremiah WARD vs William MERRITT
    -     Ezekiel SMITH vs John DINGESS
    -     Noah SCALES & wife Anne vs John REA
    -     Robert SANFORD vs Roland BIAS
pg 183    M.BOSTICK      vs W.MERRITT case $5000.00
          H.HAMPTON Jr.vs J.HOGAN      AB    3000
          E.SHELTON      vs S.SANDERS        10,000.
          S.SUMMERS      vs E.SHELTON        15,000
          J.CHADWICK     vs W.HAMPTON        3000
          B.GARRETT      vs J.BIAS           1000
          James BIAS     vs Jas.GARRET       1000
          Alex.PORTER    vs J.WARD           800
          J.WARD         vs D.DOUTHAT        800
pg 183    G.HOLLENDBACK vs T.WARD       $10,000
          EVANS & al     vs HAMPTON          298 & 200
          M.RUSSELL      vs HAMPTON               100(pounds)
          M.BOSTICK      vs W.MERRITT   ink
          T.WARD         vs HANNAN      ink
          D.RUFFNER      vs J.BARRETT
```

begining on page 187 information is for the year 1865

        This book has been used for three separate entries.
            1.Minute Book I 1809-1815 Cabell County,VA
            2.Court Minute Entries 1865-1866 Cabell County,WV
            3.An account book for 1855- Washington Aqueduct

Frequency of Jury duty Cabell County

BY YEAR   1809-1810-1811-1812-1813-1814-1815
               9990001111222223333334444455555

```
Adkins,Berry              ------11
Adkins,Hezekiah           ------1----22--------------55
Adkins,Hezekiah Jr.       ---------------------------5
Adkins,Littleberry        -----------------------4----55
Adkins,Reuben             ------------------------------5
Adkins,William            ------11----22---------4----5
Aldridge,James            ------11
Alsbury,Charles           99-00
Amos,John                 ------1----2
Barker,William            ------1--------------4
Barner,John               ---0
Barnheart,Peter           ---0
Barrett,Andrew            ------11---222--333--------5555555
Barrett,James             ---------------------44
Barrett,John              ------1111-2222-----------55555
Barrett,Joseph            ----------------3
Barrett,Samuel            ---------------------333-------55
Bartram,Stephen           ------11
Baul,Robert               ---------------------------5
Bean,Stephen              ---------------------33---4----5
Bears,James               9
Bellamy,John              ----------------------------5
Benson,Samuel             ------111
Benton,John               ----------------3
Biars,James               ---0
Bias,James                -----------------------------5
Bias,Obadiah              -----------------------4
Bias,Rolen                ----------------------------555
Black,Adam                ----------------------------5
Blake,Kenneth             -------------2----3----444--55
Blankenship,Jess          ------------------3
Blankenship,John          --------1
Blue,Samuel               9
Booth,Charles             9--0------22222222-3
Booton,Reuben             ---0--1
Bostick,Manoah            9--00------22--------------5
Boult,Isaac               -----------22
Boult,James               -----------22
Boult,Robert              --------------------------5
Bowen,Hugha               ------111
Brammer,Edward            ----------------------------5
Brown,Benjamin            ------11---22---3----44---5
Brown,Berry               ----------------3
Brown,Henry               99
Brown,Richard             ---0--11---222------------5
Brumfield,Bird            ----------------------------5
Brumfield,William         -----------22---33-------55555
Brumley,William           --------------------------5
```

```
Bryant, Lawrence        ------1----2----3--------5
Buffington, Jonathan    9
Buffington, Robert      ------1
Buffington, Thomas      9--0------------3333-44        (Sr.?)
Buffington, Thomas Jr.  ---------------------5
Buffington, Thomas Sr.  ------1
Buffington, William     ---0001111-2222------444--555
Bumgardner, Phillip     ----------------3----4----55
Burns, John             -----------------------5
Burton, John            ---0--1--------33    444445
Byers, James            ----------22
Campbell, John          ---------------33---44444
Cantril, John           ---------------------------55
Cardwell, Nathan        ---------------------------55
Carter, John            --------------------------5
Casebolt, Robert        ----------2
Catlett, Alexander      ------1
Catlett, Alexander Jr.  9---------------3
Chapman, Andrew         ----------------------4
Chapman, Cadwalder      --------------------444--5
Chapman, George         --------------------4----55555
Chapman, Thomas         ----------------------4
Childers, Thomas        --------------------4----55555
Clap, Thomas            99900011111222223333 3
Clark, Samuel           ----------------------4
Clark, William          ----------22222333--44444555
Conley, Isaac           --------22
Conner, James           ------------------------444--555
Crawford, Reuben        ----------22
Cross, William T.       ------1----2
Crump, Holly            ----------22222
Crump, Richard          ----------22---3----44
Cumings, Charles        ---------------3
Davidson, George        ------11----------4
Davis, Benjamin         ----------222--3
Davis, Daniel           ------111--2------------55
Davis, David            9
Davis, Jesse            ------------------------5
Davis, John             ------1
Davis, Paul             9
Davis, William          -------------------------5
Dempsy, William         ----------2
Denison, George         ---------------33
Dial, Ransom            ----------2------------55
Dingess, John           -------------------------55
Dingess, William        ---0
Dirting, Peter          ---00
Douthat, Daniel         ---0--1----2222------44---55
Douthat, David          9-----1
Dunbar, William         ------1
Ellis, Spencer          ------1-------------4
Estill, Zachariah       ------111--2----3
Estis, Joel             ------1---------3--------55
Everett, John           -----------222223----444--55
```

```
Everett,John Jr.        ---------------------3----4444-55
Everett,John Sr.        ---------------------33---4444-555555555
Everitt,Nathan          ----------------------------555
Everitt,Nathaniel       -------1--------------------5
Ferguson,Daniel         ----------------3
Ferguson,John           9--0--1111-222223----444--55
Ferguson,Samuel         9--0--1---------333--4
Ferguson,William        ----------------33
Ford,James              ---0
France,Daniel           -------1----222------------5
Frazure,Micager         -----------2
French,David            ----------------------4
Fudge,Jacob             ------11---2222-33
Fullerton,John          ------1111-----------------55
Fullerton,William       9--0001111-2----3333------55555
Gardner,Newton          -----------2
Garrett,Benjamin        9--0
Garrett,Benjamin Jr.    9
Garrett,Benjamin Sr.    ---------------------4
Garrett,Joseph          -----------2---------4
Garrett,Isom            ------1111-222--3-----4
Gilkerson,John          -------------------------5
Gosdon,Robert           ------1
Gray,James              ------11---2222-3
Greenwood,William       9--00------2--------444--5
Griffith,John           ---0--1----2222233---4
Guin,Andrew             -------------------------5
Hampton,Henry           ------1
Hampton,William         -----------------33---444--55
Hannan,Isom             ------11---222
Hannan,John             -------------------3--------555
Harris,John             ------1
Harrison,John           ------1
Harrison,Obadiah        ---0
Hatcher,Henry           ------------222------------55555
Hatfield,Adam           ----------------3
Hatfield,Isaac          ---00---------------4
Hatfield,John           ------11--222222333--4----5
Hatfield,Thomas         ----------------3----444--555
Hatfield,William        -----------------333--44---55555
Hatton,Asa              ---------------------4
Hayner,Fredrick         -------------------------5
Hayner,William          ----------------333
Haynie,Henry            ------11112222222223334
Hazlett,Alexander       -------------------44
Heath,Isreal            -----------22-------------5
Heily,Joseph            -----------2
Helphinstine,Henry      ---------------------4
Henry,John              --------------------4----5
Hensley,Solomon         -------------------------5
Hensley,Stephen         -----------------------444  55
Highzy,John             -----------2
Hilyard,Joseph          99-0-11111122------------55
Hinch,Samuel            -------------------------5
```

```
Hite, Jacob              ----0--11---2-----------4----5
Hite, William            ---------------------------5
Hodges, Stephen          -----------------3
Hogan, David             ---0
Hogan, James             ---0--11
Holderby, Absolum        --------------------------5
Holderby, James          9-----111122222233---4----5
Holderby, Robert         ---0--------222-------4
Holderby, William        -----------22---33----4
Holland, Michael         99-0
Hollenback, George       9----1---------------44---5
Hollenback, John         ------1----222--33
Hollenback, Martin       ------1
Hoskins, James           ------1
How, Chester             ---00-1----222-----------5
Huddleston, John         -------------------------5
Huddleston, Samuel       ----------------------55555
Huggard, Andrew          -------------------44
Irvin, John              ------------------  4
Irvin, Thomas            -------------------------5
Johnson, Perry           ----------2
Johnston, Benjamin       ------------------------55
Jones, John              ----------22
Jorden, James Sr.        9--0--1
Jorden, William          ---0-------2222
Kelly, Stephen           9
Kilgore, Thomas          9--00-1----------3----444--55
Lafoure, James           -------------------4
Leonard, Rufus           -------------------4
Long, John               ----------22
Lore, Peter              ----------2-------------5
Love, Charles            ---0
Love, Peter              ---0
Love, William            9----11------------4
Lower, Peter             99-0--1----2
Markum, Jacob            -------------------44
Markum, James            -------------------4
Markum, Stephen          ------------------------55
Markum, William          -------------------4
Martin, Benjamin         -------------------4
Maxey, Ben               -----------------3
Mayo, James              -----------2----333-------5
McColuter, Thomas        ----------------------5
McComas, David           9--00-111--2---------4----55
McComas, David Jr.       ------------------------555
McComas, Elisha          99900------2222233---4----5555555
McComas, Jesse           ------1111-22---3----4----5
McComas, John            --------------------444
McComas, Isaac           -----------------3--------5
McComas, Moses           ------1111-2----3----4----5
McComas, William         ----------222--33333444--55
McComas, William Jr.     --------------------4
McGinnis, Achilles       ------11
McGinnis, Edmund         ---00-1----2----3----44444555555
```

```
McGinnis, James          ------1----2----3---------5555
McGinnis, Phyrrus        ----------------------------5
McGinnis, Samuel         ------1---------33
McGonagle, Joseph        ------------------------444--555
McMahan, John            ------11---2----33
Merritt, John            ------111--2---------4----5
Merritt, Lerose          99-0--111
Merritt, Obadiah         ---0--1--------------------55
Merritt, William         ------------22---333--44---555
Miller, Hugh             ------11---2----3
Miller, William          ---------------------4----5
Moman, James             ------1---------33
Morgan, Daniel           -----------------333--44---5
Mormans, James           ---00
Morris, John             ----------------------------5
Morris, John Jr.         ---0--------2222-33----444445
Morris, John Sr.         ---0--1----2----------4
Morris, Thomas           --------------------------55
Morris, William          ---------------------4
Morris, William D.       ------1---------3----4
Morrison, Charles        ------1
Morrison, Patrick        ---------------------------5
Neal, Daniel             ---0
Neal, Samuel             ---00-------2
Newman, John             -------------------------5
Newman, Leroy            -------------------------4
Nixs, David              ---0
Patten, David            ---------------------------5
Pauley, Edward           ------1----------------4
Payton, Henry            ------111111-------------55
Peters, Mathew           ----------222
Peyton, Jonathan         ---------------------------5
Plyton, HUgh             ---------------------------5
Porter, Alexander        9
Poteet, James            -------------------333
Ramsey, Charles          ------------------33--------5555555
Ray, Jesse               ------------------------555
Rea, James               ---0-----------------------5
Rece, Allen              ---0-----------------------5
Rhei, James              ------1
Rich, Benjamin           -----------------------4
Rodgers, George          ------------22---33---444--5
Rodgers, John            ----- 111--22---3----4
Russell, Isaac           ---0
Russell, Jeffery         ------1----22222
Russell, John            ------1
Russell, Mark            99-0--111--2----3
Russell, Phillip         ----------22
Russell, William         ----------2
Rutherford, Robert       ------11111---------4
Sample, John             ---------------------------5
Sanders, Sampson         ------1----22---3333------5
Scales, Nathaniel        9--0--1---------3
```

```
Scales, Noah               ---------------22---33---4----555
Scales, Peter              ---0--1-------------4----5
Seamonds, Elijah           ----------------------------55555
Sharp, Leonard             -------------------3----44
Sharp, Richard             ------1
Short, Samuel              -------11------------4----5
Simmons, Elijah            ----------------------4      (Sea-)
Simmons, John              ---0-------2----3
Sires, Abraham             -------------------33
Slaughter, Goodrich        ------------22
Slaughter, Reuben          ---00--11--------------4----55
Slaughter, Robert          -----------22
Smiley, Samuel             ---------22222223333-4----555
Smith, Adam                ------------------------55
Smith, Ezekiel             ---------------------------55555555
Smith, James               -------1----2----3----4----5555
Smith, John                ------------------3----4----555555
Snodgrass, James           ------------------3----4
Sperry, Abijah             -----------22
Spiers, George             ---------------------------55
Spurlock, Daniel           ----------------------44
Spurlock, David            ------------22---3
Spurlock, George           9--00-111--2
Spurlock, Jesse            ---00------222--3----44---55
Spurlock, Stephen          ------111
Spurlock, William          ------------22---3333
Stailey, Jacob             ----------------------4----5
Stailey, Stephen           --------------------------55
Stephenson, Alexander      ------------------33
Stephenson, Benjamin       -----------2
Stephenson, Gilbert        9--0-------2----3
Stephenson, Samuel         ------------22
Stephenson, Zach           9
Stokes, Brice              --------------------4
Stroop, Malchor            ---0--11---2----3
Stuart, Charles            ------1--------33
Sullivan, Gilbert          -----------2
Swearingin, Leonard        -------------2---------4----555
Swearingin, William        -----------------------444
Terrell, Richard           -------------------4
Thompson, James            ---------------------4----555
Thompson, William          -----------222
Thornburg, Solomon         --------------------4
Toney, Jesse               ---------------------------5555
Toney, Squire              -----------2
Toney, William             ----------------------------55555
Torga, James               9
Tunkle, Henry              -----------2
Turley, James              -----------22---33---44---5555
Vaughn, Thomas             -----------22
Walker, Daniel             -----------22---3333
Walker, Patent             ------1----2----333
Walker, William            ------11---222--33---4
Wallace, John              -------------------3
```

```
Walton, William      ----------------------3333-4----5
Ward, John           -----------------------------5
Ward, Thomas         -------------2---------4
Wellman, Jeremiah    ------------------------44
Wellman, John        -----------2222------4444-5
White, James         -------------------------5
Wilson, Charles      ------------------------5
Wilson, James        ------111-------3-----444--555
Wilson, Robert       ---0--11---22
Wilson, Stephen      -----------2--------------555
Wince, Philip        9
Wishon, John         ---------------------------5
Witcher, Daniel Jr.  ------1----22---3333------5
Witcher, Daniel Sr.  -----111111-----3333------555
Witcher, Sanders     ----------------333333
Youst, Christian     ------1
```

Some obvious county residents serve little jury duty.
Reasons:1.Justices of the peace or other members of court.
        2.Platiff or defence.
        2.Tavern owners or other business owners.
        3.Came late on Court Day to miss jury duty.

Juries called each year including 2 Grand Juries.

```
            1809--3
            1810--5
            1811--16
            1812--21
            1813--15
            1814--16
            1815--27
```

Adams, Robert 15, 37, 42
Adkins, Berry 12, 13
Adkins, Hezekiah 12, 16, 21, 33, 34
Adkins, Hezekiah Jr. 34
Adkins, James 12, 21, 26
Adkins, Littleberry 12, 17, 21, 29, 33, 34
Adkins, Randel 28, 30
Adkins, Reuben 34
Adkins, William 12, 13, 16, 20, 27, 35
Aldridge, James 14, 15, 42
Alexander, Henry 42
Alherson, Spencer 40
Allen, James 12, 16, 20, 23, 25, 27, 28, 29, 32, 34
Allen, William 29, 31
Alsbury, Charles 6, 7, 8, 9, 11, 38
Amos, John 12, 21
Armstrong, John 25
Arthur, John 42
Bachgramble, Jacob 10
Baker, Abraham 27, 29
Ballard, Philip 42
Barber, Levi 22, 24
Barker, William 13, 26, 29
Barner, John 8, 13
Barnheart, Peter 8
Barnheart, Polly 6, 7, 8, 9, 39
Barrett, Andrew 12, 13, 20, 21, 22, 24, 33, 34, 35, 36
Barrett, Edward 20, 38
Barrett, James 25, 27
Barrett, John 9, 11-13, 15-21, 27-30, 33, 34, 36, 38, 40, 43
Barrett, Joseph 22
Barrett, Samuel 24, 33, 36
Bartram, Stephen 12, 13
Baul, Robert 33
Bean, Stephen 23, 24, 27, 32, 33
Bears, James 6, 7, 8
Bears, Obidiah 6, 7, 8
Bellamy, John 29, 30, 32, 33
Benson, Samuel 13, 14, 15
Bentley, George 29
Benton, John 26
Biars, James 8, 38, 39
Bias, James 33, 43
Bias, Obidiah 29, 38
Bias, Rolen 28, 30, 35, 36, 42, 43
Black, Adam 34

Blake, Kenneth 16, 21, 23, 24, 25, 28, 30, 31, 33-36
Blankenship, Archibald 34, 35
Blankenship, Jesse 21, 23, 26, 28, 30
Blankenship, John 11
Blue, Samuel 8
Booth, Charles 6, 8, 17-19, 25, 37, 40, 41
Booton, Reuben 8, 12
Bostick, Manaoh 6-8, 10, 12-19, 22, 24-28, 34, 39, 43
Boult, Isaac 18, 19
Boult, James 21, 37
Boult, Robert 32
Bowen, Hugha 13-18, 21-23, 26, 33, 34
Brammer, Edmund 30, 32
Brammer, Edward 28, 32
Brammer, Henry 28, 30
Brammer, John 28, 30, 33
Brook, Benjamin 43
Brown, Benjamin 10, 12, 16, 20, 25, 27, 29, 32, 35
Brown, Berry 23
Brown, Henry 6, 7, 9, 10, 19, 38
Brown, John 26, 28, 37
Brown, Richard 8, 12, 13, 15, 17, 19, 34, 38, 40, 41
Brumfield, Bird 35
Brumfield, Micajah 23, 28, 29, 32, 35
Brumfield, William 18, 19, 24, 25, 32, 33, 35, 41, 42
Brumley, William 32, 33
Bryan, James 24
Bryant, Lawrence 9, 12, 16, 17, 25, 34
Bryson, Edmund 38
Bryson, Rebeckah 38
Buffington, Jonathan 6, 10, 13, 40, 41
Buffington, Robert 14
Buffington, Thomas 6, 8, 12, 15, 22-25, 29, 37, 40, 42
Buffington, Thomas Jr. 11, 31
Buffington, William 8, 9, 11, 13, 16, 18, 19, 23, 25, 27, 29, 31, 33, 34, 37, 40, 41, 42
Bumgardner Phillip 26, 29, 32, 36
Burcham, James 17
Burcham, John A. 22
Burcham, John 17, 22, 25, 27, 29, 32, 35, 41, 42
Burns, John 35

Burns,William 33
Burris,William 35
Burton,John 8,10,23,25-32,35,
    36,42
Byers,James 10,12,13,16-18,20,
    21,24,40,41
Byers,John 10,13,21,40,41
Campbell,John 24,26,28,29,31
Cantrill,John 33
Caperton,Hugh 22,42
Cardle,Edward 12
Cardwell,Nathan 36
Carter,John 34
Cartmill,David 6,7,22,23,25,26
Casebolt,Robert 20
Catlett,Alexander 11,16,20,22,
    24-26,30,38,41
Catlett,Alexander Jr.7,8,22,
    24,25
Catlett,Horatio 11,16,19,23,
    25,41
Cavendish,William H. 7
Chadwick,John 42,43
Chafin,David 28,29,32,35,41
Chafin,John 28,29,32,35
Chambers,John 23
Chandler,William 17,20,23
Chapman,Andrew 31
Chapman,Cadwalder 27,30,34
Chapman,George 29,32,33,35,42
Chapman,Thomas 7,9,28,30,31,39
Childers,Joseph 19
Childers,Thomas 31-34
Clap,Thomas 6-14,16,18,19,21,
    23-29,40
Clark,Samuel 27
Clark,William 17,19,20,24,26,
    28,30,31,33,34,43
Coalter,John 6,7,8,9
Coffee,Peter 10,13,17,21,41
Coleman,William 26,28
Collins,Lewis 30
Conley,Isaac 18,21,24
Conley,Thomas 33
Conner,James 31,33,36
Cook,John Sr. 42,43
Cordeman,Christian Fredrick 42
Cornwell,Wesly 12
Counts,George 34
Cox,John 10,17,22,26,28,30,33
Crawford,Reuben 18,19
Creedle,Edmund 14,15
Cresson,James 27,28
Cripon,James 27,28

Cross,William T.15
Crump,Holly 10,11,16,18,19,
    20,25
Crump,Richard 6,7,9,10,16,17,
    19,20,23-29,32,35,37,38,
    39,41,43
Cumings,Charles 23
Cushing,Nathaniel 34
Davidson,George 11,12,15,16,25,
    27-29,34,40,41
Davis,Benjamin 17,23,27,37
Davis,Daniel 14,16,18,23,31,
    34,36
Davis,David 7,12,13,19
Davis,George 16
Davis,John 11
Davis,Paul 23,30,31
Davis,William 12,14,20,32
Dempsey,William 21
Denison,George 24,25
Dial,Ransom 20,35
Dickinson,Adam 19
Dingess,John 32,35,42,43
Dingess,Peter 25
Dingess,William 9,29,31,33,35,
    40-43
Dirting,Peter 8,21-23,27,29,
    32,34,38,40
Donnally,Andrew 10,11
Douthat,Daniel 8,9,12,17,20,
    27,30,34,36,40,41,43
Douthat,David 6,40
Douthat,Robert 25-27
Dreadnot,Ferdinado 10,11,12,16,
    23,26,30,36,37
Drown,Nancy 6,7,8,9,37,39
Dunbar,William 10,18,40
Dundass,John 12,16,18,22
Dundass,L.17
Duvall,Nancy 12
Ellis,Spencer 12,27,28
Estill,Zachariah 10,15,17,19,
    26,28,31
Estis,Jack 12
Estis,Joel 10,26,28,30,34,
    36,40
Evans,H.16
Evans,Richard W.20,25,27,29,
    32,35,36,41,42
Evans,Thomas 7,8,9,10,27,35,
    39,40
Everett,John 16,18,19,22,26,
    27,29,34,36

Everett, John Jr. 24, 26, 28, 29, 31, 36
Everett, John Sr. 25, 31-34, 36, 42
Everett, Nathan 34, 36
Everitt, Nathaniel 34
Fair, Phillip 10
Fairplay, Phillip 18, 28, 30, 33
Fannin, John 37
Farler, Henry 37
Farley, Henry 32, 37
Ferguson, Jane 7, 9, 39
Ferguson, John 6, 8, 9, 12-14, 17, 19, 20, 24, 25, 29, 30, 35, 36, 40, 41
Ferguson, Samuel 6, 8, 10, 13, 17, 21, 23-25, 30, 31, 40, 41
Ferguson, William 8, 23, 25
Ford, James 8
Forth, John 12
France, Daniel 10
France, Henry 12, 25, 40, 41
Franklin, Edward 33, 35, 42
Frazer, Hastin 33, 35, 42
Frazure, Micager 21, 25
French, David 31
Fudge, Jacob 9, 13, 18, 19, 21, 23, 25, 41
Fullerton, James 36
Fullerton, Jane 6, 7, 8, 39
Fullerton, John 12-15, 35, 38
Fullerton, William 6, 8, 11, 12, 16, 21, 23, 24, 27, 29, 32, 34, 36, 38, 40, 41, 42
Gaines, Herbert P. 20
Gallaher, James 42, 43
Gardner, Newton 18
Garrett, Benjamin 6, 8, 20, 27, 43
Garrett, Benjamin Jr. 8, 20, 26
Garrett, Benjamin Sr. 30, 31
Garrett, Isom 6, 7, 12, 13, 16, 21, 23, 27
Garrett, James 43
Garrett, Joseph 10, 16, 23, 24, 27, 30, 31
Garrett, Robert 42
Gilkerson, John 32, 33
Gosdon, Robert 12
Gray, James 9, 13, 17, 19, 24
Greenwood, William 6-8, 12, 16, 19, 21, 30, 31, 34, 39
Griffith, John 8, 17, 19, 20, 21, 23, 27, 40
Guin, Andrew 34
Hager, James 41
Hairston, George 22, 25, 28, 30, 31
Hall, Martin 8
Hammer, Fredrick 15, 20, 22, 23
Hampton, Henry 7, 9, 10, 14, 15, 20, 21, 24-27, 39, 40, 43
Hampton, William 23, 24, 26-33, 42, 43
Hanger, James 32, 35
Hannan, Isom 9, 11, 12, 20, 21
Hannan, John 8, 9, 10, 11, 26, 32, 33, 38, 39, 40, 43
Harbour, David 10, 12, 17
Harmon, John 12
Harrison, John 12
Harrison, Obadiah 8
Hatcher, Henry 17, 20, 22, 32, 33, 35, 37
Hatfield, Adam 25, 36, 42
Hatfield, Isaac 8, 28, 38
Hatfield, John 9, 12, 17-20, 23-25, 27, 35, 42
Hatfield, Thomas 24, 31, 35, 36, 42
Hatfield, William 26, 28, 29, 35, 36, 42
Hatton, Asa 23, 26, 30, 31
Hayner, Fredrick 33
Hayner, Mary 33
Haynie, Henry 10-13, 16-25, 28, 29, 31, 34, 40
Haynie, William 24, 25
Haze, Andrew 16
Hazelwood, Pleasant 37
Hazlett, Alexander 29-31
Heath, Isreal 18, 19, 32, 35-37, 42
Heily, Joseph 19
Helphinstine, Henry 28
Henderson, James 17
Hendrick, Jacob 28, 31
Henley, Samuel 27
Henry, John 16, 29-32, 34-36, 41
Henry, Samuel 28, 29, 30
Hensley, Daniel 22
Hensley, David 24
Hensley, Solomon 35
Hensley, Stephen 13, 27, 18, 31, 35-37
Hepburn, William 12, 16, 17, 19, 22
Hephinson, James 41
Highzy, John 19, 21
Hilyard, Joseph 6-9, 12-15, 18, 19, 34, 35
Hilyard, Thomas 30
Hinch, Samuel 35-37, 42
Hite, Jacob 9, 12, 17, 26, 28-31, 34, 40, 41

Hite,William 34,42
Hodges,Stephen 26
Hogan,David 8
Hogan,James 7-11,14,15,20,
    38-41,43
Holderby,Absolum 33
Holderby,James 7,10-13,15,16,
    18-25,29,32,35,41,42
Holderby,Robert 8,10,16,19,22,
    23,29,40
Holderby,William 6,7,15,18-20,
    22-25,27,37,38,40
Holland,Michael 6,7,9
Holland,Sarah 7,9,39
Hollenback,George 7,12,27,29,
    34,39,43
Hollenback,John 10,13,17,21,
    24,26,40,41
Hollenback,Martin 13,40,41
Hopkins,Samuel M.30,31
Hoskins,James 11
How,Chester 6-9,11,12,15,16,
    18-22,25-27,34,36,39
How,Nancy 9,15,16,18
Huddleston,John 33,35,36
Huff,Thomas 31
Huggans,Samuel 10,13,17,21,23,
    26,27,29,40,41
Huggard,Andrew 31
Hunter,Henry 6
Hurley 32,36
Hutchinson,Isaac 7
Irvin,Thomas 8
Jack,Jeremiah B.12
Jackson,Jeremiah B.15
Jackson,John 22,24
Janney,John 42
Johnson,Benjamin 36
Johnson,Joshua 42
Johnson,Perry 18
Johnson,Pattsey 42
Johnston,Pierson 12,13,14,16,
    25,27,28,40
Jones,John 18,19
Jones,Joshua 6,7,8,24,28,30,39
Jordan,Andrew 6,7,8
Jordan,Charles 29,33,42
Jorden,James Sr. 7,9,12
Jorden,William 6,8,12,17,21,
    38,39
Kelly,Beal 21
Kelly,Greenberry 24,25,28,30,
    34,36

Kelly,Stephen 6-8,10,16,18,
    23,25,34,35,42
Kilgore,Thomas 6-9,12,26,29,
    31,32,34,38,39
Lafoore,James 29
Laidley,John O. 27,35
Lee,J.40
Lee,John 10,11
Leonard,Rufus 31
Lockheart,Bird 22,24
Lockheart,James 7,9,10,27,30,
    35,36
Long,John 12,16,18,19,29,31
Lore,(Love)Peter 21,32
Love,,Charles 9,31,40
Love,William 8,10,12,29
Lovell,Joseph 27,34
Lower,Peter 6,7,8,12,21
Madison,James 10,18,22,26,28,
    31,33
Manazer,Claudius R.22,24,31
Markum,Jacob 31
Markum,James 29,31
Markum,Stephen 32,33
Markum,William 29
Martin,Benjamin 29
Mathers,John 36
Maxey,Ben 26
Mayers,James J. 9
Mayo,James 21,23-25,32
McClung,William 26,28,37
McColuter,Thomas 34
McComas,David 6,8,9,12,13,21,
    23,31,35,36,38,40
McComas,David Jr.32,33
McComas,Elisha 6-9,16,17,19,
    20,22-24,26,28-30,33-36,
    38,40-42
McComas,Isaac 25,35
McComas,James 23
McComas,Jesse 9,13-15,17,23,35
McComas,John 29,30,31
McComas,Joshua 23
McComas,Moses 12,13,20,23,
    35,42
McComas,Richard 23
McComas,Sarah 23
McComas,Thomas 9,32,35
McComas,William 20-25,27,30,
    31,35,36
McCormack,James 26
McCormack,Joshua 26
McCormack,Rachael 26

McCormack, Sarah 26
McCormack, Moses 23, 26, 28, 29
McCown, Mathis 31, 38
McGinnis, Achilles 14, 15
McGinnis, Edmund 6, 8, 9, 12, 15,
    16, 19, 22, 23, 25, 26, 29,
    31-34, 36, 37
McGinnis, James 12 12, 19, 26,
    34, 36
McGinnis, Lewis 42
McGinnis, Milly 42
McGinnis, Phyrrus 34
McGinnis, Samuel 12, 26
McGonagle, Joseph 29, 30, 34,
    36, 42
McGonangle, James 36
McMahan, John 9, 12, 16, 20, 22-26,
    34, 43
Meeks, John 28, 30, 32, 35, 41
Merritt, George 37
Merritt, John 9, 12, 16, 20-22,
    29, 33
Merritt, Lerose 6-8, 13, 15, 16, 23
Merritt, Obadiah 6-9, 12, 15, 18,
    21, 24, 26, 27, 29, 30, 32-35,
    39-41
Merritt, William 6-13, 15, 21-29,
    31-33, 36, 38, 39, 43
Merritt, William Jr. 38
Miller, Edward 43
Miller, Hugh 10, 12, 13, 17, 22, 27,
    40, 41
Miller, James 38
Miller, William 29, 35
Moman, James 7, 8, 12, 19, 26, 27,
    37-39, 41
Morgan, Charles 17
Morgan, Daniel 17, 23-29, 34
Morgan, Elizabeth 23, 26, 28
Morgan, Simon 17
Mormans, James 8, 12
Morris, Edmund 6-8, 10-12, 16, 17,
    19, 20, 23, 25-27, 31, 34, 37, 42
Morris, John Jr. 8, 9, 17-29, 31,
    34, 36, 38-41
Morris, John Sr. 6, 7, 9, 12, 27, 40
Morris, Peggy 7
Morris, Sally 7
Morris, Thomas 32, 34, 42
Morris, William 9, 119, 20, 27, 41
Morris, William D. 10, 25, 29
Morrison, Charles 12
Morrison, Patrick 36
Morrison, William 17, 23

Mott, Moses 10, 13, 17, 40, 41
Munsey, Samuel 42
Neal, Daniel 8, 10, 12, 13, 17, 18,
    27, 34, 40, 41
Neal, Samuel 8, 15, 19, 21, 22,
    26-28, 31
Neal, Thomas 10
Newman, John 35
Newman, Leroy 28
Niell 32
Nixs, David 8
Ousley, David 42
Page, Carter 26, 28, 30, 32, 34, 36
Parker, Alexander 29
Patten, David 35
Pauley, Edward 11, 30, 31, 33, 35, 42
Payton, Agatha S. 10, 32
Payton, Garrett 10
Payton, Henry 12, 13, 14, 15, 36
Payton, John H. 10, 32
Payton, Susannah S. 10
Perry, William 37
Peters, Mathew 21, 22
Peyton, Jonathan 36
Plyton, Hugh 36
Poage, George 27
Porter, Alexander 6-8, 38, 43
Poteet, James 10, 13, 17, 18, 21,
    24, 26, 41
Pratt, William 42
Preston, Thomas L. 8, 16
Prior, Allen 27
Prior, Harry 32, 35, 42
Ramsey, Charles 24, 26, 31-36, 42
Ray, Jesse 36
Rea, James 8, 32, (Ray) 36
Rea, John 43
Rece, Allen 8, 34
Rece, Edward 42
Rece, James 31
Reynolds, John 9, 10, 15
Reynolds, Maurice 27
Reynolds, Richard 36, 42
Rhea, Edward 18, 21, 24, 26, -29,
    32, 35, 41
Rhei, James 16
Rice, James 26, 27, 28, 30
Rich, Benjamin 31
Riggs, Stephen 40
Rodgers, George 10, 13, 16, 17, 19,
    23-25, 28-32, 36, 40-42
Rodgers, Jane 42
Rodgers, John 6-11, 13, 16, 21,
    24, 28, 31, 34, 39

Rose 12
Ruffner,Daniel 9,15,16,20,
    27-30,33,36,39,40,43
Ruffner,Joseph L.9,15,27-30
Russell,Isaac 8,13,14
Russell,Jeffery 12,14,15,17,
    18,19
Russell,John 6,8,9,18,22,24,40
Russell,Mark 6,7,9-16,25-28,31,
    34,37,38,40,43
Russell,Philip 19,20
Russell,William 20,26,27
Rutherford,Robert 9,10,12,13,
    15,23,26,28,30,31
Sample,John 35
Samuels,John 24,37
Samuels,Joseph H.27,35
Sanders,Martha 12,18
Sanders,Sampson 9,13,18,19,
    23-25,34,39,40,41,43
Sanford,Robert 43
Scales,Anne 43
Scales,Nathan 20
Scales,Nathaniel 7,9,10,13,15,
    16,19,23,38,31,34,40
Scales,Noah 9,15-20,22,23,25,
    26,29,32-35,43
Scales,Peter 8,16,27,32,34
Scott,Robert G.28
Seamons,Elijah 33,36
Seekright,Ammadab 10-12,16-19,
    22,23,26,28,30-32,34,36,
    37,42
Sharp,Leonard 26,27,29
Sharp,Richard 11,25
Shelton,Elizabeth 39,43
Shelton,James 40
Shelton,John 9
Shelton,Samuel 22,25,28,30,31
Short,Samuel 6-11,15,16,22,23,
    25,27,28,30,32,33,38-40
Simmons,Elijah 31
Simmons,John 6-12,16,18
Simmons,Sally 28,32,36
Sires,Abraham 23,25,26
Skinner,William 22,24
Slaughter,Ezekiel 10
Slaughter,Goodrich 18,19,30,
    35,36
Slaughter,Reuben 7-9,15,16,29,
    30,35,36
Slaughter,Robert 18,19
Smiley,Samuel 9,16,18,19,21-24,
    27,31-34,37

Smith,Adam 32,35,37
Smith,Ballard 7,12
Smith,Benjamin 42
Smith,Ezekiel 32,33,35,36,43
Smith,Ginny 36
Smith,James 12,20,24,29,32,
    33,36
Smith,John 26,29-32,34-37
Smith,Joseph 26,28,30
Smith,Susannah(Payton) 10
Snodgrass,James 25,30
Southerland,Alexander 35,42
Sperry,Abijah 21
Spiers,George 36
Spiers,Henry 35,36,37,42
Spurlock,Burwell 12
Spurlock,Daniel 30,31,34
Spurlock,David 9,10,16,19,22,
    26,30
Spurlock,George 7-9,12-14,16
Spurlock,Jesse 7-9,16,18,20-22,
    25,27,29,34,38,40,41
Spurlock,Stephen 9,12,13
Spurlock,William 19-24,40,41
Stailey,Jacob 29,35
Staley,Stephen 33
Stephenson,Alexander 26-29,31,
    32,35,41
Stephenson,Benjamin 18
Stephenson,Elijah 28,29,32,35
Stephenson,Gilbert 8,16,18,26
Stephenson,Samuel 20,21,37
Stephenson,Zach 8
Stevenson,James 10
Stokes,Brice 11,15,29,41
Stone,John 35,37,42
Stribling,Edward S.12
Stroop,Malchor 8,12,13,22,26,37
Strother,Agatha(Payton)10
Stuart,Charles 10,13,16,23,24,
    34,35,40,41
Stuart,James 43
Stuart,John 18,21,24
Sullivan,Gilbert 17
Summers,G.43
Summers,Lewis 7
Swearingin,Leonard 18,29-34
Swearingin,William 29,31
Tabor,Robert 6,37,38
Taylor,Allen 9
Taylor,Charles 10
Terrell,Richard 28,31
Thompson,James 31,33,36

Thompson, Squire 32, 35
Thompson, William 17, 18, 19
Thornburg, Solomon 29
Tiernan, John 42
Toney, Francis 28, 31
Toney, Jesse 32, 33
Toney, Squire 19
Toney, William 7, 32-34, 37-39
Torga, James 8
Tull, R. 40
Tunkle, Henry 19
Turley, Arthur 26, 30, 32
Turley, James 7, 18, 20-22, 24, 26,
   29, 31, 33, 40
Vaughn, Reuben 12, 14, 15
Vaughn, Thomas 31
Walker, Charles 34
Walker, Daniel 21, 23-25, 27, 31,
   33, 34
Walker, Patent 9, 20, 24-26
Walker, William 8, 11, 13, 18-20,
   23, 25, 30, 31, 34, 42, 43
Wallace, John 25, 36, 37
Walton, William 24, 27, 29, 31, 33
Ward, George 10, 11, 13, 16-19, 25,
   26, 31, 34, 40, 41, 43
Ward, Jeremiah 6, 9, 19, 26, 28, 31,
   34, 36, 37, 42, 43
Ward, John 16, 18, 20, 22, 26, 28-31,
   36, 37
Ward, Samuel 31
Ward, Thomas 6-13, 15, 16, 18-43
Watson, James T. 23, 26, 28, 30, 31
Wellman, Jeremiah 30-32, 35, 36,
   39, 40
Wellman, John 21, 23, 25, 27, 31, 32
Wheatley, Richard 26, 27, 28, 31
White, Benjamin 42
White, Henry 16, 34, 35
White, James 33
Whitecotton, Patsy 10, 13, 40, 41
Wilburn, Sally 33
Wilks, James 10, 17, 21, 23, 25, 27,
   29, 40, 41
Wilson, Charles 36
Wilson, James 6-8, 12, 13, 16, 22,
   24, 25, 27, 31-34, 37, 38, 42
Wilson, John 20, 22
Wilson, Robert 8, 12, 13, 18, 20, 42
Wilson, Stephen 19, 32-34, 36,
   37, 42
Wilson, Thomas 28
Wince, Philip 7
Windon, Joseph 29

Wishon, John 35
Witcher, Daniel Jr. 10, 12, 13,
   17-20, 22, 24, 26-30, 32, 37,
   40, 41
Witcher, Daniel Sr. 6, 12-16,
   19-22, 24-26, 32-34, 36, 38,
   40, 42
Witcher, Sanders 10, 12, 13, 17, 20,
   23-25, 27, 35-38, 40, 41
Wood, David J. 42
Wood, Simmon M. 18
Woodward, John 7, 9, 10, 27, 36
Woodward, Silvester 7
Youst, Christian 16
SLAVES
-Charlotte 13
-David 13
-Harris 13
-Patsy 13
-Peter 7
-Phebey 13